THE
LITTLE
BOOK
OF
RANELAGH

MAURICE CURTIS

First published 2017

The History Press Ireland
50 City Quay
Dublin 2
Ireland
www.thehistorypress.ie

The History Press Ireland is a member of Publishing Ireland,
the Irish book publishers' association.

British Library Cataloguing in Publication Data.
A catalogue record for this book is available from the British Library.

ISBN 978 0 7509 8361 7

Typesetting and origination by The History Press
Printed and bound by TJ International Ltd.

Front cover image: The Hill pub, Old Mount Pleasant, Ranelagh.
(publin.ie)

CONTENTS

Acknowledgements   5

Introduction   6

1. Early History – The Massacre of
    Cullenswood and the Bloody Fields   11

2. The Village of Ranelagh and the Triangle   18

3. The Forgotten Village of Cullenswood –
    Beechwood to Sandford   34

4. From the Heart of the Revolution to
    Dunville Village   61

5. Looking to the Stars – Ranelagh
    Road and Dartmouth   73

6. Old Mount Pleasant, the Square and
    Hell's Kitchen   88

7. 'Through the Barrier Please!' – Waterways,
    Tramways and Transport   99

8. The Devil's Kick – Churches and Schools   106

9. Parks, Pundits and Sport   117

10. From the Parlour to Pinocchio –
    Food Glorious Food   127

11.   'Drink! Drink! Drink! To eyes
        that are bright ...'   135

12.   Stop the Lights! – Still More Luminaries   139

        Further Reading   144

ACKNOWLEDGEMENTS

A special thanks to Terry Connaughton and all in the Ranelagh Arts Office, to the De Courceys for information on Beechwood Avenue Parish, to Beechwood Avenue Parish and to Sandford Parish Church; Donal Fallon of comeheretome.com for information on Mount Pleasant; Drew Cooke of DCC; publin.ie for photo of the Hill pub; Graham Hickey of Dublin Civic Trust and the Irish Architectural Archive. Grateful thanks also to all the shops, businesses and schools in Ranelagh (RMDS and Scoil Bhríde, Lios na nÓg, Gonzaga and Sandford Co-Ed). Dublin City Council on many fronts (including its Parks Department) has undertaken sterling work in the Ranelagh area and this has to be acknowledged. To the Ranelagh, Rathmines and Rathgar History Society and to the various residents associations, thanks a million! I am also indebted to Susan Roundtree and the late Deirdre Kelly for their very important and vital research and work on Ranelagh's history and heritage. Shamrock Rovers FC was very helpful also on the subject of their time in Glenmalure Park. Staff and owners at McSorley's, Humphreys, Smyth's, The Hill and Birchall's Pubs, Redmond's and Gammell's were kindness itself. The DCC libraries and in particular the staff of Rathmines Library and Pearse Street Archives were very helpful. Special thanks to all the kind businesses and residents of Ranelagh.

INTRODUCTION

Ranelagh is situated approximately two miles south of Dublin city centre, bordering the Grand Canal, between Rathmines to the west and Donnybrook to the east. It is served by the Luas Green Line and a number of Dublin bus routes and is about a twenty-minute walk to and from the city centre.

The name 'Ranelagh' is of relatively recent vintage in terms of being applied as the name of this historic area. It replaced the older name of 'Cullenswood'. In fact, the area was known as Cullenswood for generations but by an accident of history it assumed the name Ranelagh. Luckily, the original name survives in certain place names in this fascinating suburb.

Ranelagh contains a delightful mixture of all kinds of roads and houses dating from the late eighteenth century onwards, including lanes of cottages, two- and three-storey-over-basement Victorian and Edwardian red-bricks and also a few detached mansions. Dartmouth Square was not completely built until the 1890s, thereby filling in some of the last remaining fields in the area. The focal point for much commercial and social activity, at the centre of Ranelagh is 'the Triangle', previously called 'the Angle', on the junction of Ranelagh Village and Charleston Road.

TWO VILLAGES AND FINE HOUSES

Ranelagh has many fine Victorian streets such as those surrounding Mount Pleasant Square, and some of its oldest houses are alongside the famous pub 'The Hill'. Ranelagh Gardens and Toole's Nurseries occupied much of the land of present-day Ranelagh from the 1770s until the end of the nineteenth century. There was also Cullenswood Village and a hint of Ranelagh Village in the early days of its development. Consequently, before it transformed into an area of orderly roads and houses, the wider area was one of fields, with a few winding paths, one or two main roads, scattered houses, farmhouses and the detached houses of the wealthy. These latter included Willbrook House, Sallymount House, Cullenswood House, Elm Park House, Belmont House, Anna Villa, Woodville House, Coldblow House, Sandford Hill, Sandford Grove, Merton House, Selskar House and Thomas Ivory's house at Old Mount Pleasant. Over time the villages of Ranelagh and Cullenswood evolved and the surrounding fields were replaced by a web of streets that make up the modern Ranelagh. Important factors in the evolution and development of present-day Ranelagh were the effects of the Great Famine on Dublin and the establishment of the Rathmines Township.

Ranelagh in 1870s. (Courtesy of Ordinance Survey Office of Ireland/UCD Map Library)

Ranelagh in the early 1870s, showing the Mount Pleasant area. (Courtesy of Ordinance Survey Office of Ireland/UCD Map Library)

FROM TOOLE'S NURSERIES TO THE TOWNSHIP

Within a few years of its establishment, Ranelagh was incorporated into the Rathmines Township and the area consequently benefited from improved roads, low rates, and a splurge of house-building. According to Professor Mary Daly, in her study of the growth of Victorian Dublin, it was probably no coincidence that Rathmines Township was established in 1847 when the Great Famine was at its peak, or that a record number of families moved to the suburbs, including Ranelagh, during the 1860s, a decade marked by epidemics of smallpox and cholera. The establishment of the township greatly encouraged more people to move out of the city. Townships were like small towns, each with their own town hall (e.g. Rathmines town hall) and commissioners (today called councillors). They were entrusted to look after issues such as roads, lighting, sewerage, drainage and water. With the creation of the Rathmines Urban Township in 1847, ostensibly, because of the poor state of the roads, the demand for houses by Dublin's middle classes (mainly Anglo-Irish Protestant and unionist), who sought a safe and healthy environment and a home that was sufficiently close to the city to commute by walking, grew exponentially. They also saw in the township an opportunity to preserve the Protestant unionist way and view of life, i.e. their identity, particularly at a time when the growth of Irish nationalism was challenging their set view.

An 1859 copy of the *Dublin Builder* noted of the burgeoning township, that 'the green sward gave way in almost fairy-like rapidity to macadamised roads and populous thoroughfares'. The affluent residents of the independent township looked after their own interests, better served under their stewardship than under the Dublin Corporation, which Sir Edward Carson described as 'a sort of Greenwich Hospital for Nationalist wrecks'.

'Nationalist Wrecks' and the Cosmopolitan Village

Consequently Ranelagh, like Rathmines and Rathgar, was predominantly Protestant, unionist and middle class. This remained the case until the 1930s, when owners started moving farther from the city centre and parts of the area began to be transformed into 'flatland'. These houses had been expensive to maintain, as the owners had only managed to do so for decades with cheap domestic labour. Even despite the fact that, from the early twentieth century onwards, modern labour-saving devices replaced domestic servants, some of the original owners sold up and moved out. However, in the closing decades of the twentieth century, change was again in the air, as people sought residences nearer the city centre, offering a certain quality of life, and started to move back into the area. The 'flatland' of Ranelagh (where old houses were converted to flats) and nearby Rathmines was slowly changing. Various residents' associations, e.g. the Beechwood Residents Association, were very active in campaigning against houses being turned into bedsits and flats.

Ranelagh has been described as one of the trendiest and most cosmopolitan villages in the city and it is home to some the best restaurants and bars in town. Quaint boutique shops, a host of supermarkets, numerous fine restaurants and pubs, two Luas stations, an artistic tradition and hub, a central position to town and a slew of top junior and senior schools, all make this position absolute prime. The land of 'red-bricks and shabby chic', someone once noted. Again, someone else has described Ranelagh as 'D4 for the trendier and edgier'. Take what you will from that!

1

EARLY HISTORY – THE MASSACRE OF CULLENSWOOD AND THE BLOODY FIELDS

VILLAGES, TOWNLANDS AND BARONIES

The district originally consisted of two tiny villages – Ranelagh and Cullenswood – and in ancient times was part of a Gaelic district called Cuala. An important road ran from the old medieval city of Dublin through Cuala to Wicklow and was known as the Dublin Way or Bealach Dubhlinne. The land in the area was part of the demesne of St Kevin's Parish owned by the Archbishop of Dublin.

The townlands of Ranelagh North and Ranelagh South were in the civil Parish of St Peter's and in the barony of Uppercross. They were bounded on the north by Harcourt Road and Adelaide Road, on the east by Sussex Road and an old irregular boundary from there to Chelmsford Road, on the south by Chelmsford Road, Ranelagh Village, Charleston Road, Oakley Road and Dunville Avenue, and on the west by Beechwood Park, Belgrave Square East, Mountpleasant Avenue Upper, Bessborough Parade, Rathmines Road Lower and Richmond Street South.

Ranelagh is in the local government electoral area of Pembroke/Rathmines, which was reconfigured as Rathgar-Rathmines Local Electoral Area with effect from May 2014. For many years, it was located in the Dáil constituency of Dublin South-East, which was renamed Dublin Bay South with effect from the 2016 General Election. Interestingly, in the important 1918 General Election, Ranelagh/Rathmines broke the nationalist trend in evidence nearly everywhere else and returned the unionist MP, Sir Maurice Dockrell.

Cullenswood: Gabriel Beranger sketch of Cullen's Castle, near Cullen's wood in 1772. (Courtesy of National Library of Ireland)

FAMOUS BATTLES

1209 – *The Massacre of Cullenswood*

It has been suggested that were it not for the Dublin and Wicklow Mountains the history of Ireland might have been different! For it was there that the Irish clans lived, in an area completely inaccessible to marauders and protected from the new invaders. These mountains had for centuries stymied the full extension of English rule beyond the Pale. The Pale or paling, an *ad hoc* fortification around mainly Dublin, was designed to prevent attacks but did little to improve matters. Consequently, following the Norman invasion of the late twelfth century, Cullenswood, situated between the seat of English power in Ireland, Dublin Castle, and the Dublin Mountains, was a dangerous no man's land where many a battle was fought between the native Irish who had been banished to the mountains and the settlers who had usurped their lands.

On Easter Monday, *c.* 1209, the infamous Massacre of Cullenswood took place. The site of the massacre was between Cuala or Cualann woods, and not too far from present-day Mount Pleasant Square and the Grand Canal. The new settlers had been enjoying an open-air celebration which involved playing 'hurling the ball' when they were set upon by the O'Tooles and the O'Byrnes and hundreds of them were killed. The settlers commemorated the massacre annually for many years as 'Black Monday'. Every year the citizens of Dublin would march with the members of the various trade guilds, dressed in battle array and carrying black flags warning the Irish tribes that they were not for turning.

In 1316 the O'Tooles attempted a repeat attack but were repelled. It was not until nearly 300 years later that the power base of the Irish clans began to succumb. In 1599 the head of Phelim O'Toole was presented to Queen Elizabeth. His rule and sphere of influence in the Wicklow area had also included what is today the Powerscourt Demesne. The queen bestowed this forfeited property on Richard Wingfield, O'Toole's nemesis. Despite that, the O'Tooles, the O'Byrnes and other Wicklow clans, under the leadership of one infamous Michael Dwyer, never gave up the battle and as late as the 1798 Rebellion continued to harass and maraud the lands of the invaders.

The Bloody Fields and Cromwell

Parts of Ranelagh, such as Sandford Road, Edenvale Road and Mountpleasant Avenue, which were just fields and lanes of Cullenswood in the mid-seventeenth century, were on the outskirts of the infamous Bloody Fields, which stretched from what later became Edenvale Road to Baggot Street and Palmerston Park. Some of these roads were pivotal for the strategic movement of soldiers and cavalry during the Battle of Rathmines in August 1649, a battle that changed the course of Irish history.

It was in that vicinity also, on ground stretching roughly from Belgrave Square to the Beechwood Avenue Church site, that the Marquis of Ormond had established his main camp overlooking Dublin prior to the disastrously significant Battle of Rathmines, when his summary defeat by Colonel Michael Jones secured for Oliver Cromwell the vital 'beach head' he needed to invade Ireland. The battle saw the combined Irish confederate and royalist forces of Ormond defeated by parliamentarians under the command of Jones. This facilitated the landing in Dublin (at Ringsend)

of Oliver Cromwell and precipitated his subsequent reconquest of parts of the country. This reconquest involved the 'to Hell or to Connaught' policy and was devised with the help of one William Petty, who had come to Ireland with Cromwell, and was based in the Crow's Nest in Temple Bar, Dublin. Within a decade, this ruthless dispossession and transplantation policy saw the ownership of the land of Ireland by the Irish fall quickly and dramatically from 60 per cent to 20 per cent by the late 1650s. The implementation of that draconian policy was undertaken in an attempt to destroy the Irish once and for all.

The Norse, Wicklow and London Connections

The name 'Ranelagh' derives from the Irish 'Gabhal Raghnaill' (with a possible Norse influence and pronounced 'Gaval Rannal'), an area in the Wicklow Mountains stretching south to Shillelagh and north to Carlow and centred around Ballinacor/Glenmalure. Until the early seventeenth century, this region was under the control of the O'Byrne family. Fiach MacHugh O'Byrne (d. 1597), a military genius and strategist, and one of the last great defenders of Gaeldom, was known in the sixteenth century as O'Byrne of Gabhal Raghnaill or Lord of Ranelagh, which reflected the clan's control of that part of Leinster. However, following the defeat of the O'Byrnes and the seizure of their lands, that title went to Sir Roger Jones, who in 1628 was ennobled as Viscount Ranelagh. His son Richard was created Earl of Ranelagh in 1677 and his London residence was called Ranelagh House. When that was sold, the site was converted into a fashionable spot called Ranelagh Gardens, the same site upon which the Chelsea Flower Show is hosted today.

WILLBROOK HOUSE

The Importance of Willbrook House

Meanwhile, back in Dublin, in the area now known as Ranelagh, a fine dwelling called Willbrook House, on the site of today's park, Ranelagh Gardens, was playing its part in the growth of a village. The house was in existence decades before Rocque's Map of Dublin for 1753 and 1762, both of which show this house on grounds with extensive gardens. The popular Dublin newspaper of 1753, *Pue's Occurrences*, described the house in a 'for sale' ad as 'held under the See of Dublin, containing 6 acres on which stands a convenient dwelling house with a view of the city, harbour, sea and Wicklow Mountains ... and a walled garden at the bottom of which is a fine canal with a considerable stock of carp and tench ... the parks are remarkably rich. A handsome avenue bounded with a canal leads to the house, the distance from Dublin is one mile on the road leading to Milltown'.

The house was previously owned by the Protestant Archbishop of Dublin and later Sir William Usher of Donnybrook was associated with it. Still later, another bishop, William Barnard, Bishop of Derry, overseer of the richest diocese in Ireland, lived there. He also held a seat in the Irish House of Lords on College Green, which is why he had a house in Dublin. It was located adjacent to the main road from Dublin to Milltown and was called Willbrook. Part of its significance lies in the fact that the village of Ranelagh subsequently grew up around it and the famous Ranelagh Gardens.

Fireworks and Dublin's 'Golden Age'

When Barnard died in 1768, a businessman, church-organ specialist and harpsichord maker, William Hollister, decided to move into Willbrook and develop its grounds as an open-air place of public entertainment in Dublin. With this in mind, he chose to emulate the premier London example by naming the 6-acre venue 'Ranelagh Gardens'. Thus, in 1769, began an exciting and action-filled twenty years centred around Willbrook and Ranelagh Gardens which saw the movers and shakers, the very upper echelons of Irish society in politics and business, attend grand and impressive balls, parties and celebrations. Huge fireworks displays rounded off the spectacle, with all the festivities taking place around the artificial lake derived from the River Swan running through the grounds. This decision to build the pleasure gardens coincided with and was part of the golden age of Dublin – the closing decades of the eighteenth century when the city was regarded as the second city of the British Empire. This was the era when the impressive buildings, wide streets, and squares of Dublin were built and laid out.

The Four Courts, Dublin.

This was the time which saw the building of the new Four Courts, the Irish Houses of Parliament (now Bank of Ireland) on College Green, the Royal Exchange (now City Hall) on Cork Hill, Newcomen's Bank (now the Rates Office) across from it, and many other landmark buildings. This was also the time when the building of the quays was nearing completion, when plans were afoot to transfer the Custom House further downriver to its present site and a new bridge linking Westmoreland Street and the new Drogheda Street (later Sackville and now O'Connell Street) was built. It was a period of enormous expectations and confidence shared by many of the ruling élite in Dublin. Having the lifestyle commensurate with this 'golden age' was *de rigueur* for those involved in the transformation of the city. Dining, wining and partying to excess were a particular feature of this era and Ranelagh played its part.

Prancer the Dancer and the Making of an Archbishop

One of those often in attendance at the 'fireworks' parties in Willbrook and Ranelagh Gardens was John Hely-Hutchinson (1724–94), politician, businessman and provost of TCD, known as 'the prancer' for his agility, style and love of dancing. His Dublin house was in Blackrock – Frascati House. Even the king, George III, was impressed by this ambitious fellow and noted (although some commentators claim it was Lord North who made the statement) that even if he gave him England, Scotland and Ireland, he would still want the Isle of Man as a cabbage garden. The Hely-Hutchinson family had an illustrious history, and one branch of the family continued in business until well into the twentieth century. James Joyce celebrated their stationery shop on Dame Street in *Ulysses*. One of the family, Charles Wisdom Hely, lived in Rathgar in Oakland House, which is now part of the St Luke's Hospital complex. The initials 'CWH' can still be seen carved and welded onto the entrance gates on Orwell Park.

Another famous person associated with dancing at Willbrook was the future Catholic Archbishop of Dublin, Daniel Murray. While a young student in Dublin, he, like so many others, had heard of the high life associated with the gardens and took leave from his studies to experience such festivities first hand. He later confided this to the Carmelite nuns who took over Willbrook when the gardens and house had lost lustre.

Get Thee to a Nunnery or Up, Up and Away!

In 1788, a Carmelite order of nuns was established on the site and the convent remained home to the nuns for nearly 200 years until the end of the twentieth century. They were an enclosed order and, in keeping with their rules, had to ensure that their faces were never seen by the public. If you wished to talk to any of them you had to speak through a grille. They used the surrounding lands as a small farm with poultry, cows and a large kitchen garden. During the War of Independence, the convent was raided by the Black and Tans, who were so thorough in their search that in the course of looking for guns and ammunition they dug up a grave of a recently buried nun. Due to declining vocations and the modernising changes ushered in by the Second Vatican Council, the convent eventually closed in 1975. The land was subsequently sold and the house was demolished in the 1980s. A reminder of the convent's presence today is a monument, sited near the Chelmsford Avenue entrance to the park, with a granite cross which was on the original chapel attached to the convent. Today's park, on the site of such contrasting historical events and tenants, is called Ranelagh Gardens – a reminder of that interesting history. The park occupies only a section of the original estate and is located on its southern part. There you'll find an imaginative statue of the young Richard Crosbie, who made aeronautic history in the late eighteenth century.

Richard Crosbie's balloon flight in 1785. (Courtesy of National Gallery of Ireland/DCC)

2

THE VILLAGE OF RANELAGH AND THE TRIANGLE

VILLAGES AND TOWNLANDS

Ranelagh Village developed from the late eighteenth century onwards. The actual village is not shown on John Rocque's Map of Dublin for 1760. However, it appears on Taylor's 1816 Map of Dublin. As was often the case in the vicinity of a castle or 'big house', the village of Ranelagh evolved in the vicinity of Willbrook House. Facilitating the many needs of Willbrook and the surrounding estate and gardens, village life developed slowly from the late 1760s onwards. A map of the area from 1837 shows Ranelagh divided into two areas: Ranelagh North and Ranelagh South, which corresponded with the villages around Willbrook and Cullenswood/Sallymount/Anna Villa, respectively. Fifty years later, when looking at a map of Ranelagh from the early 1870s, one can clearly see the separation of the two villages that constituted the area we know today. The map shows Ranelagh Road extending from Charlemont Bridge over the Grand Canal and to the village outside the gates of Willbrook and the junction at the Angle. From then onwards the road shown on the map is called Cullenswood Road and extends from the Angle to what is now Marlborough Road. Then the road becomes Sandford Road, extending from that junction to Belmont Avenue opposite Milltown Park. Four distinct townland names subdivide the area into Ranelagh North, Ranelagh South, Sallymount and Cullenswood.

Late-eighteenth- and early-nineteenth-century terraces overlooking the growing village, as well as being part of the transformation, include Mander's Terrace, Selskar Terrace and Old Mount Pleasant. On the opposite side and further into the village, some of the old houses on the east side, near the present-day Luas bridge, date from the 1760s (particularly some along by Dowling's towards the Ranelagh Arts Centre, nos 2–18). These eclectic houses are perched precariously along a crazy misshapen-looking terrace. The opposite side of the road, from nos 3 to 27, is a much more uniform terrace, with two-storey houses of a later, late-nineteenth-century/early-twentieth-century vintage. Businesses occupy the ground-floor levels of these red-brick houses.

SHOPS AND BUSINESSES

Small Shops, a Bustling Village and 'Pure Air'

There was a time when there were many small shops – crafts, dairies, bakeries, hardware stores, chandleries – as well as various services and businesses in Ranelagh. The vast majority of them have disappeared in the last few decades, yet the buildings they occupied remain the same – just with different tenants.

Few will recall the old Turkish baths, near the entrance to the convent under the railway bridge, yet it was part of a long-gone but short-lived era in Dublin. There is a reminder of this era on Dublin's O'Connell Street – the Hammam Buildings, which was the site of the former Hammam Hotel and the location for Dublin's first Turkish bath. It was built in the 1860s and survived until it was destroyed in 1922 during the Civil War. There was also Turkish baths in Rathmines, known as the Rathmines Oriental Baths, towards the end of the nineteenth century. A newspaper ad at the time was addressed to: '... the inhabitants of Rathmines, Ranelagh, Rathgar and the south suburbs of Dublin': 'The Rathmines Oriental Baths enjoy the benefit (not attainable in a central position in a large city) of an unlimited supply of Pure Air, which is very essential to the renovating and invigorating effects of the Bath'. The most popular Turkish baths in Dublin at the time was the one at Lincoln Place, next door to the Café de Paris, the first French restaurant in Dublin.

Some old businesses have survived, including a barber's shop, Oakline Furniture (1958), Ranelagh Cycles, McCarthy's shoe shop and, until recently, Dowling's shoe-repair shop. Redmond's, a legendary off-licence emporium, is likewise one of the few old family businesses still trading (and thriving) in Ranelagh. Humphreys Pub is another, with the same family still running the business more than a century later! Meagher's Pharmacy, which has two branches in Ranelagh, first opened in Baggot Street in 1921 but was sold to the present owner Oonagh O'Hagan in 2001. She trained under the guidance of Pierce Meagher and so the tradition continues. The Ranelagh Road branch is also on the site of a previous pharmacy.

Ranelagh and environs from John Rocque's Map of Dublin, 1760. (Courtesy of UCD Map Library)

Cabaret and Night Owls

Years later in the 1960s and '70s, a popular music and cabaret venue sprang up along the terrace, facing the Triangle. This was known at various times as the Chariot Inn, the Richard Crosbie Tavern, and finally, the Four Provinces, with Night Owls nightclub downstairs. Joe Dolan celebrated his 36th birthday during his Saturday-night cabaret stint at the Chariot Inn. When the venue had Night Owls, it claimed to be 'Europe's only laserdisc nightclub' and it had an ad on the radio extolling its virtues:

> Night Owls, it's the place to be seen,
> Night Owls, the Disco's cool as a dream,
> Night Owls, bars open late with music that is great,
> Why go to the rest?
> When Night Owls is the best!

At one time, it boasted four bars and the band Who's Eddie used to play there at weekends. It survived until 1999 when Superquinn (now Supervalu) bought it. The nightclub reopened as the short-lived

Il Mundo, sporting a bouncy dancing floor and often finishing a rave night with 'Old Red Eyes' by Beautiful South or 'Rock da House' by Tall Paul.

THE DARLIN' OF DUBLIN

Ken Doherty is one of the most talented and successful snooker players ever to have picked up a cue. He is also the only player ever to win the Under-21 Amateur and World Snooker Championships. It was at Jason's Snooker Rooms around the corner from where he lived on Ranelagh Avenue that the future snooker ace Ken Doherty learnt and honed his skill from a very young age. In fact, such was his determination and love for the game that he had to stand up on a biscuit tin to try to reach the balls when he was a young lad. Coached by the former Irish international, Paddy Miley, the young Doherty found he had a natural talent with the cue and entered various amateur competitions. In 1989, at the ripe old age of 20, Doherty won the World Amateur Championship and was duly invited to become a professional of the game.

Four years later, after losing his first Grand Prix to Jimmy White, Ken went on to win his first ranking title, the Welsh Open, which was enough to catapult the 'Darlin' of Dublin' to the top sixteen players in the world. Doherty etched his name in the record books in 1997 by winning the World Championship using a cue he bought in Jason's. He was only the third player from outside the UK to win the World Championship at The Crucible and he did so by beating Stephen Hendry 18–12 in the 1997 final. Returning to Ireland a hero, Doherty would go on to play in two more World Championship finals and stay in the top sixteen for over a decade. His snooker club, Jason's, was demolished in 2012. But Doherty is still going strong, with, amongst other things, a snooker academy in Terenure, next to Brady's Pub.

A famous billiards hall known as Rosimars operated in the village from 1907 to 1986. It survived from the days when billiards was more popular than snooker and operated behind Ryan's shop, a newsagent which sold clay pipes and Peggy's leg (like a stick of rock).

MORE SHOPS AND BUSINESSES

Other old and long-gone shops in the area included Slobber Maher's (where Supervalu is now), Daly's bicycle shop, the Monument

Creamery, P.J. Kilmartin's Turf Accountants, the Kylemore, Keegan's Fishmonger and Grocer, Ranelagh Seed and Plants and Alex Findlater's. The last of these was renowned for its whiskies and wines (and teas for many years) and had been trading in Dublin since 1823. The business traded as Findlater Wine Merchants from the old whiskey-bonded vaults under the Harcourt Street railway station.

The Chandlery, the Swastika and Redmond's

Opposite the present-day Ranelagh Arts Centre and Supervalu is what was once MacGowan's Terrace, with numbers 1–29. All the old photographs of Ranelagh show Gordon's Chandlery and Ironmongery at the corner where Spar is today. The old photos also show the horses, cabs or 'outside cars' as they were called, and cab drivers waiting for a fare, right in the centre of the Triangle. The Triangle itself seemed to have trees and shrubs surrounded by railings. One hundred years later, modern cabs and taxis are still waiting for fares.

The Dublin Laundry Company and Dartry Dye Works were next to Gordon's. Prescott's was also in Ranelagh. Battery-driven laundry vans, such as those of the Swastika Laundry and the Kelso Laundry, were a frequent sight in Ranelagh for many years. Redmond's is one of the few surviving old family businesses still *in situ* and thriving since 1945. It was said that at one time 'you could buy your whole dinner there'. There was a similar off-licence business in the same premises since 1900. The off-licence was originally also a grocer's shop, run by Mary and Jim Redmond. 'Everything was sold loose out of bins, and we bottled the Guinness ourselves', recalls their son Jimmy, who, along with his brother Aidan, now runs Redmond's of Ranelagh, the only Dublin off-licence to win the coveted National Off-Licence of the Year Award (NOFFLA) – twice!

The Butcher, the Baker and Jaunting Cars

Shops may have changed hands but the line of the terrace remains the same. Both sides of the road in the vicinity of the Triangle are replete with shops that originally sprang up in tandem with the growth of the village. Some old names not forgotten include Myles McDonnell's dairy, Gordon's Chemists, Johnston Chemists, Stanley Wilson Chemists, Cosgrave Butchers (still thriving in the village of Rathfarnham) and Kelly's Butchers. Then there were Keegan's fish and poultry shop, Gilbey's Wine Importers, Field's jaunting car maker, Russell's pub, O'Sullivan's grocery, Astra Travel, Wit's End Boutique and Magno's Chipper. Further along from the Triangle, towards the Sandford Road, we had the Spotless Cleaners and the former HCR Chemist's. Leech's and Meagher's Chemist are still *in situ*, however. McSorley's Pub has the word 'chemist' on the mosaic floor at the main entrance. At least the present owners are still maintaining the tradition of dispensing health-inducing concoctions!

'A Tradition Made Fresh Every Day'

McCambridge's Bakery had a shop in Ranelagh for decades (at no. 35 and on the corner with Elmwood Avenue). Besides selling soda bread, it also provided ice cream and chocolate made in the shop. It opened in 1945 when Malcolm McCambridge moved from Shop Street in Galway to start a business in Dublin. The Galway shop still thrives to this day. His son, John, later took over the business. Initially selling products sourced from around the world, he gradually developed a range of local produce made with the help of a team located in the kitchen just behind the store. Recognising the increasing popularity of McCambridge home-made foods, John took the opportunity to market them nationally. Steadily, the Irish stoneground wholewheat bread ('a tradition made fresh every day') increased in popularity and managed to capture a one-third share of the Irish market. The packaging has the signature of John McCambridge on it. The shop in Ranelagh closed in 1985. The business continued to flourish in bigger premises elsewhere and more than twenty-five years later was selling an average of 160,000 loaves per week, a terrific achievement.

Many of these old businesses have now been replaced by cafés and restaurants that line the main thoroughfare, such as Tribeca, Cinnamon and others that keep changing their names (or tenants), although Mario's Restaurant has been in Ranelagh for more than twenty-five years. Wong's was burnt down after being in Ranelagh for many years, on the site of the old Sandford Cinema. Three big supermarkets have replaced the small family groceries, and concentrated around the Triangle – Spar, Lidl and Supervalu.

THE ANGLE AND THE TRIANGLE

Configuring Ranelagh

This site was constructed in the mid-1850s and was originally called the Angle as the new road from Rathmines approached Ranelagh at an angle to avoid the Methodist church (since demolished), which jutted out at the end of Oakley and Charleston roads. It later became known as the Triangle, which may have been due to the configuration of the path or to the fact that three roads converged there, giving the appearance of a triangle. Some will recall the old red-bricked public toilets in the very centre of the triangle and the taxi rank that surrounded it. The area where the Ranelagh Credit Union now stands was originally called Field's Terrace and has changed very little in nearly 150 years.

At the side of what was once Russell's pub is Westmoreland Park, a terrace of cottages and a reminder of the old village of Ranelagh. The entrance faces the Triangle and contains old cottages huddled together along a straggling line. Also, hidden away, on the opposite side, near the angle where Charleston Road and Oakley Road meet the Triangle, are Moran's Cottages, a group of cottages dating from around 1900. Like Westmoreland Park, these are nearly invisible to the casual passer-by, but may be accessed through a narrow arch. It is quite difficult to believe that these two little and nearly invisible enclaves are of a different era, yet are so near to the hustle and bustle of the Triangle and the Ranelagh thoroughfare.

Monument to Deirdre Kelly

Located on the Triangle is a memorial to conservationist and local historian Deirdre Kelly, who wrote the definitive history of the wider area in her landmark book, *Four Roads to Dublin*. The memorial is a modern silver-coloured pyramid-like structure. Deirdre was a lifelong local historian *par excellence*. She was also a radical conservation and environmental activist and a founding member of the Living City Group, which aims to save Dublin's heritage in its many guises. Consequently, she was involved in numerous campaigns to preserve Dublin's rich and diverse historic fabric and architectural heritage. She featured strongly in both the Hume Street and Wood Quay battles, the first for Georgian heritage and the latter for the Viking influences on the early development of the city. She was also a founding member of the Rathmines, Ranelagh and Rathgar Historical Society. *Four Roads to Dublin* is a detailed and illuminating account that examines the rich layers of history, the architecture, the lore and the growth and development of a distinctive and dynamic area of Dublin that is one of the most important eighteenth-century parts of the city. Everything is explored with the utmost diligence and affection. Deirdre Kelly died in 2000 and the fitting memorial was unveiled in her honour at the Triangle in 2009. Her words are written on this memorial and reflect all that was good about her and her deep appreciation for Ranelagh, for Dublin, for our natural and built heritage – the legacy of our past that must be preserved. After all, we are just stewards of our wonderful kingdom. In her own words:

> Wherever one walks one is conscious that these are living streets steeped not just in their own history but woven into the history of Dublin. Writers and musicians, unionists and nationalists, scientists, poets and artists lived – and still do – in the houses which line the streets.

POLITICS, PERSONALITIES AND THE PDS

Chairman and Chief-of-Staff

The Triangle has also played an important role in the careers of local politicians. Former Tánaiste and Minister for Justice Michael McDowell lives in Ranelagh, and not too far from the Triangle. He is the husband of Professor Niamh Brennan of the UCD School of Business. Professor Brennan's many achievements include being the chairman of the Dublin Docklands Development Authority, establishing the UCD Centre for Corporate Governance, and being the director of many state and private bodies and organisations. She is also chairman of the National College of Art and Design. McDowell is a senior counsel, a former politician and a founder member of the Progressive Democrats political party in the mid-1980s. He is a grandson of Professor Eoin MacNeill (1867–1945), scholar, Irish language enthusiast, co-founder of the Gaelic League, founder and chief-of-staff of the Irish Volunteers and Sinn Féin politician. On three occasions, McDowell was elected as a TD for the Dublin South-East constituency (now called Dublin Bay South, which includes Ranelagh), serving in the 25th Dáil (1987–89), the 27th Dáil (1992–97), and the 29th Dáil (2002–07). He lost his Dáil seat at the general elections of 2007.

During his distinguished years in public life, McDowell also served as attorney general of Ireland (1999–2002), as minister for justice, equality and law reform (2002–07), as leader of the Progressive Democrats (2006–07), and as Tánaiste (2006–07).

Panto Time – Chance Would be a Fine Thing in Ranelagh

The course of Irish history might have turned out differently had it not been for a 'chance' meeting of two local politicians at the Triangle in 2007. It was during the election campaign of May of that year that the public witnessed the taking-off of the leather gloves when McDowell and Green Party leader John Gormley clashed verbally at Ranelagh's Triangle. Onlookers, photographers, reporters and TV cameras had gathered around Mr McDowell at the Triangle for his press briefing. As part of it, he was unveiling a poster saying 'Left Wing Government? No Thanks'. As was his tradition when it came to poles and posters, he mounted a ladder, put up his election poster and posed for the scrambling photographers. It was said that he was taking his party's fight for political survival to the street of his own constituency in the very heart of Ranelagh.

Demise of the Generals

However, the political stunt seemed to backfire, or maybe not, as suddenly, and seemingly out of the blue, onlookers were treated to a clash on the street between rivals. McDowell's constituency rival, Green Party chairman John Gormley, arrived on the scene and the two men engaged in a verbal spat. Gormley wanted McDowell to reject a Progressive Democrats pamphlet which the Green candidate claimed was false. Mc Dowell kindly advised Gormley to 'calm down' while other PD members told him to go away, but Mr Gormley replied, 'It is you who is finished'. Gormley repeatedly requested McDowell to admit that the political pamphlet was awash with lies. Just as the razzmatazz was about to finish, another Dublin South-East candidate, Lucinda Creighton of Fine Gael (and later of Renua), arrived to put up a poster of her own.

Was it an ambush or mere coincidence that the two rivals should just happen to be in the same place at the same time? There was much speculation that Ireland would be treated to a Green/PD coalition government. People were not taken in by the seemingly heated exchanges between supposed rivals behaving like generals preparing for battle. However, all enjoyed the political nonsense about raising taxes, lies and smear tactics. 'Sure, haven't they to come on stage every so often and give us a bit of a pantomime', opined one Gaiety Theatre panto stalwart. Eventually, everyone decided to give up on politics and retire to the nearest snug.

Bikes, Emissions and a Chinese Takeaway

The clash of rivals at the Triangle worked on the PR front for the participants, whatever their motives. The incident fronted the evening's main news. The outcome was that Gormley was re-elected, beating McDowell for the last seat by 304 votes. Following his party's victory, Gormley led the negotiations with Fianna Fáil about forming a government. On 14 June 2007, he was named as minister for the environment, heritage and local government in the new coalition. In that position he introduced many pieces of legislation and measures aimed at reducing energy consumption and harmful emissions/pollutants in order to protect the environment. In 2009 he launched the highly successful 'bike scheme' to encourage cycling to work.

In his leader's speech to the Green Party conference in April 2008, he provoked the Chinese ambassador and diplomatic delegation into walking out by calling for solidarity with the people of Tibet and referring to Tibet as a nation.

The Final Countdown for the PDs and the Resurrection Shuffle for the Greens

Pundits have speculated whether that clash marked the end of both the Progressive Democrats and the Green Party. The 2007 General Election was a disastrous one for the PDs, with Michael McDowell and others losing their seats, leaving the party with only two TDs. They had gone from a high of fourteen TDs in 1987 and had been part of a coalition government with Fianna Fáil. After conceding his seat to John Gormley at the RDS count centre in Dublin, McDowell abruptly resigned as party leader and announced his immediate retirement from public life. He has since resumed his private legal career. The party disbanded in 2009. The Green Party was also subsequently annihilated in the 2011 General Election, as a result of the public's ire over the collapse of the Celtic Tiger economy. Gormley lost his seat, as did the other five TDs. Eamon Ryan succeeded him as leader of the Green Party. After a few years in the wilderness, the party fought back and now has a few TDs in Dáil Éireann, promoting the Green agenda. In the 2016 General

Election, Eamon Ryan won a seat for the Greens in the Dublin Bay South constituency.

Meanwhile Michael McDowell had no intention of taking a back seat, despite his removal from the immediate political arena – Dáil Éireann. In 2013 he clashed with Education Minister Ruarí Quinn over the future of the Seanad during a debate organised by the Ranelagh Arts Festival and held at Sandford Park School. The voters rejected the proposal on the abolition of the Seanad. McDowell had campaigned against its abolition. He returned to politics in 2016 and was elected to Seanad Éireann on the National University of Ireland panel.

THE RANELAGH ARTS FESTIVAL

Ranelagh Arts Centre is the headquarters of the Ranelagh Arts Festival and has become an important and permanent feature in the village in recent years. The centre has its origins in the 2005 festival, which continues every September, when a group of local enthusiasts recognised the importance of Ranelagh in so many areas of Irish life, and not only in literature. They decided to do something positive about it so that Ranelagh and the wider community would benefit and grow, with the arts as a rallying and invigorating point. In 2009 the group found a home in its current space at 26 Ranelagh, from which they run a year-round programme of exhibitions, live music, poetry readings, creative workshops, cine clubs and any number of other creative activities designed to connect the community (local and beyond) with artistic and cultural opportunities. Committed to providing a platform and incubation environment for creative and community activities, the centre is a key locus of information for the promotion of the arts. It is supported by Dublin City Council, the Arts Council and the local business community, and crucially underpinned by an enthusiastic group of volunteers who look to the stars.

The annual festival programme features local artists and musicians, performances by children from the area, poetry, plays and film, as well as internationally recognised artists. Since its establishment, the festival has included luminaries such as Maureen O'Hara, Neil Jordan, Liam O'Maonlaí, Frank McGuinness, Donal Lunny and Ken Doherty, to name just a few, in its line-up. The ever-popular Walks and Talks are also an indispensable feature of some of the excellent work organised by this dynamic group.

EARLIER POLITICS AND PERSONALITIES

The Notorious Major and the Assassins

Just beyond the Triangle end of Ranelagh Village going towards Sandford Road are Elmwood Avenue and Elm Park Avenue, both on the right-hand side of the road. Here we are in the vicinity of the former grounds of Elm Park House, the entrance of which faced towards present-day Chelmsford Road. This old house was said to have been that of the notorious Major Henry Charles Sirr (1764–1841), a member of the Dublin Volunteers, later the Dublin Fusiliers, a police officer, a wine merchant and collector, who resided there from the early 1800s to the 1820s. He also had a number of other properties in the immediate vicinity stretching up to Sandford Road and Cullenswood. Very useful indeed, as at least three assassination attempts were made on him.

1798, Pitch-capping and the 'Man from God Knows Where'

Originally from Golden Lane/Bride Street in the Liberties, Sirr was from a military family and his father was attached to Dublin Castle. After a stint in the army, he returned home to his wine business on Mercer Street. He was involved with Dublin's Merchants' Guild and from there became involved with Dublin Corporation. In 1796 he joined the Dublin Volunteers and in the same year was appointed town major and then marched into Irish history.

It was he who made herculean efforts to crush the Irish Rebellion of 1798 and was responsible for the arrest of Irish revolutionaries Lord Edward Fitzgerald, General Thomas Russell (known as 'the man from God knows where' because the people in Belfast couldn't understand his Cork accent) and Robert Emmet. It was he who supervised and encouraged the use of pitch-caps and floggings on any disaffected citizens, and there were many. Pitch-capping was a particularly torturous method of punishment involving pouring boiling pitch or tar into an upturned cone and then pressing it down on the victim's head while at the same time binding the arms of the victim. The Royal Exchange (now City Hall) at Cork Hill was used as a headquarters by Major Sirr and from there he organised the wholesale arrest, torture and execution of many of those involved in 1798. In fact, murder was the favourite pastime of Sirr and the militia. He was instrumental in implementing the government's draconian response to the 1798 Rebellion in Dublin.

From Croppy's Acre to Ranelagh

The chief topics of conversation among the well-to-do in Dublin were the hangings, shootings and burnings – such was the extent of the ferocity and the cruelty exacted. Several of the lamplighters were hanged from their own lampposts for neglecting to light the lamps. Every morning the dead were exhibited in the yard of Dublin Castle. They were displayed and then unceremoniously dumped in a mass grave in what is now known as Croppy's Acre along the north quays of the River Liffey.

Sirr was detested by the citizens of Dublin for his heavy-handed approach to law enforcement and had come to live in Ranelagh for safety. In fact, Sirr became the most hated man in Dublin. In 1808 he became a police magistrate and for many years after continued to mete out his variety of justice to the arrested. He was buried in the churchyard of St Werburgh's Church, while one of his victims, Lord Edward Fitzgerald, was buried in the vaults inside.

Zozimus and the Young Irelander

Near Sirr's house, at the end of the street on the left, a Lutheran minister performed 'Gretna Green'-style marriages in the eighteenth century, and the famous street singer Zozimus (Michael Moran, known as the 'Bard of the Liberties') is reputed to have performed at these ceremonies.

From the 1850s onwards, Elm Park House was occupied by the Rev. Benson, founder of the Rathmines School. His family and a number of boarders also resided in the house. Around 1900 the house was demolished and the red-bricked houses on Elm Park Avenue were built.

The Young Irelander Charles Gavan Duffy lived at no. 4 Elm Park around 1850, the year the wealthy stockbroker John Goold died. The latter had also lived along here and was responsible for the very fine church on Zion Road, Rathgar, having left a large sum of money for it in his will.

THE TWENTIETH CENTURY

Guests of a Nation and Boxing the Fox

Across the Ranelagh Road from Elmwood Avenue and Elm Park Avenue is Chelmsford Road, leading to the Appian Way and Leeson Street. This long and winding road was laid out from the early 1860s to the 1890s. It developed on a site of 'Kavanagh's Field'. This road, together with the Appian Way and Sallymount Avenue, linked two of the four old roads into Dublin city.

Rose Skeffington, the mother of pacifist Francis Sheehy Skeffington, who was summarily executed during the 1916 Rising in Portobello Barracks, lived in no. 36. The renowned novelist and short-story writer Frank O'Connor (1903–66), who wrote the classic *Guests of a Nation*, lived for a time in no. 34. As well as sitting on the board of the Abbey Theatre, being a teacher and a librarian and taking an active part in the War of Independence and Civil War, O'Connor was also a literary critic, essayist, travel writer, translator, poet and biographer. The story of *Guests of a Nation* is set during the Irish War of Independence and chronicles the doomed friendship between the members of an IRA unit and the two British Army hostages whom they are guarding.

O'Connor's early years are recounted in *An Only Child*, a memoir published in 1961, which has the immediacy of a precocious diary. US President John F. Kennedy made an anecdotal reference to *An Only Child* during the conclusion of his speech at the dedication of the Aerospace Medical Health Centre in San Antonio on 21 November 1963:

> Frank O'Connor, the Irish writer, tells in one of his books how, as a boy, he and his friends would make their way across the countryside, and when they came to an orchard wall that seemed too high and too doubtful to try and too difficult to permit their voyage to continue, they took off their hats and tossed them over the wall—and then they had no choice but to follow them. This nation has tossed its cap over the wall of space and we have no choice but to follow it.

ART FOR ART'S SAKE

Gerard Dillon and the Connemara Landscape

In nearby Chelmsford Avenue, the prominent, enormously talented and prolific artist Gerard (aka Gerald) Dillon (1916–71), lived in no. 28. He was a landscape and figure painter who liked to work in the west of Ireland. His discovery of the area, while on a cycling holiday in 1939, was described by James White of the National Gallery of Ireland 'as the most important event in his life'. The imagery of the land, criss-crossed as it was by stone walls and dotted with cottages, and of the people in their brightly coloured home-spun clothes, remained with him for life and reappeared in many of his works. Dillon was interested as much in the life of the people as in the landscape. His Connemara works are atmospherically memorable, showing people working the land. His style was often expressionist, abstract, autobiographical and surreal. His style of painting is personal and idiosyncratic, deriving inspiration from the work of Gauguin, Chagal and Seán Keating – a sort of magic realism, with dreamlike landscapes and interiors peopled by farmers and fishermen but also Pierrots and strange hallucinatory figures. He was a highly regarded painter and his works were often shown at the Royal Hibernian Academy. He represented Ireland at the Guggenheim International Exhibition. James White wrote a book on Dillon and said, 'it is hard to imagine that any other artist ever got more out of his art than Gerard did. Through it he discovered the full joy of creativity.' Hanging in the National Gallery of Ireland is a self-portrait of Gerard, as well as a landscape of the west of Ireland. When he died, the Arts Councils of Belfast and Dublin set up an exhibition with 104 works, which consisted of oil, watercolour, collage, tapestry, mixed media and etching. His painting of the 'Black Lake' was also selected by the Irish Post Office for their fourth stamp.

Ranelagh, the 'Ulster Group' and the Paycock

Dillon greatly encouraged and collaborated with a few artists, including George Campbell (1917–79) and Arthur Armstrong (1924–96); the latter shared a house with him. Campbell was a particular friend of his and he and his wife Madge later bought a house in Ranelagh, just down the road at no. 2 Florence Terrace (Leeson Park Avenue). The Campbells had originally lived in a flat at 42 Oakley Road in the late 1940s. His tapas and music sessions at Florence Terrace were renowned, particularly after the pubs closed. George was one of the founders of the Irish Exhibition of Living Art (1943) and wsa particularly fascinated by the Spanish and bohemian characters. He produced abstract paintings based on both Spanish and Irish landscapes. He was an impressive and professional flamenco guitarist. The Spanish government conferred on him the honour of knight commander in 1978. He made stained-glass windows for Galway Cathedral and wrote books including *A Guide to the National Monuments of Ireland* (1970).

Arthur Armstrong's work was influenced to an extent by cubism and the School of Paris style, reflected in his landscapes and still-life works. Like Dillon, the textures, colours and shapes of the west of Ireland inspired some of his finest work.

Dillon, Armstrong and Campbell were all from Belfast and had travelled the world, eventually settling in Dublin. They were part of the 'Ulster Group' of distinguished artists from Northern Ireland. In 1969, the three designed the set for the Abbey Theatre's production of Seán O'Casey's *Juno and the Paycock*. It is quite extraordinary that three of Ireland's most eminent artists of the twentieth century should have lived in such close proximity and in Ranelagh. They brought a progressive sense of purpose to the Dublin art scene from the 1940s onwards and according to Brian Fallon 'were in the vanguard of Irish art in the post-war years'.

Florence Terrace – Staging Post to Stardom

Florence Terrace itself has been described as 'a quiet dog-shaped cul-de-sac just off the Appian Way'. The official name today is Leeson Park Avenue, yet the old name, Florence Terrace, is still on a house wall. The famous actress and comedienne Rosaleen Linehan (b. 1937), spent a number of her childhood years in no. 5. Amongst her many achievements was RTÉ's *Get an Earful of This*, which was a satirical radio programme. The father of George Bernard Shaw, George Carr Shaw, lived in no. 21 and the actor Patrick Bedford lived in no. 4.

Most of the original houses on nearby Winton Road were demolished to make way for the tennis club. One of the former residents was Senator Eoin Ryan of Fianna Fáil.

Dancing and the First Dáil

Chelmsford Lane was the home for many years of the Ranelagh Boxing and Social Club. Dances (the precursor to discos) were held in the club regularly and locals recall that consequently patrons ended up as expert boxers and dancers and sometimes they confused the two at the weekly dance.

Facing the Fitzwilliam Lawn Tennis Club on Appian Way is the fine big red-bricked corner house of no. 12. It was here that Michael Collins found refuge during the War of Independence. It had a secret room accessible through a hidden opening in a wall just at the turn of the staircase. Ten feet deep, 3.5 feet high and 4 feet wide, it could hold up to six people at a push. The house also played an important role in Ireland's history at the time: the Cabinet of the First Dáil met there and members of the GHQ of the Irish Republican Brotherhood also held their meetings in the house.

3

THE FORGOTTEN VILLAGE OF CULLENSWOOD – BEECHWOOD TO SANDFORD

CULLEN'S WOOD CASTLE

For historian and conservationist Deirdre Kelly, Cullenswood 'was the village that disappeared from the maps'. The area derived its name from the Gaelic word *Cuala* or *Cualann*, which referred to lands of the Colon or Cuala or Cualann, comprising hundreds of acres of fields and a 66 acre wood. Barley and grain were grown here and the quality of Cuala ale was renowned. Following the Norman invasion at the end of the twelfth century, the lands of Cuala were transferred to the ownership of the Norman Archbishop of Dublin. To complicate matters further, there was a castle in the area known as Cullen's Wood Castle, built by the Normans to deter the native Irish who had been evicted from Dublin and the surrounding lands and were now entrenched in the Dublin and Wicklow Mountains.

Old maps also show a few houses in the vicinity of Cullenswood where a village had developed around the medieval Cullen's Wood Castle. Consequently, Cullenswood is the older part of Ranelagh, with Ranelagh Village only developing centuries later with the building of Willbrook House and the opening of the Ranelagh Gardens. With the expansion of the wider Ranelagh area from the 1830s onwards, the two villages eventually coalesced. Yet, the name Cullenswood Road was still shown on maps of the area as late as the 1870s. The Rathmines Town Commissioners were instrumental in dropping the Gaelic-derived name Cullenswood. This is not surprising, however, given the unionist influence on the town hall.

The name Cullenswood has not been completely obliterated and reminders are still to be found in the immediate area, with Cullenswood Park just off the Sandford Road and Cullenswood Gardens off Merton Drive. At no. 96 Ranelagh, opposite Humphreys Pub, there is a further reminder high up on the wall. Here an old address sign boldly states: 'Feigh-Cullen Buildings'. Furthermore, the road sign for Oakley Road is given in Irish and it gives us some idea of the area's history – Bóthar Feadha Cuileann, which sounds more like an Irish version of Cullenswood. The Forgotten Village of Cullenswood

FROM THE PRONTO TO PARADISE

Toole's Nurseries was one of the largest businesses in Ranelagh from the late eighteenth century, covering nearly 30 acres and mainly supplying trees to all the fine gardens attached to the big houses, including Willbrook. The Ranelagh Seed & Plant Shop was a favourite with local gardeners from the 1940s. Mackey's was another.

Other prominent businesses here included the Pronto Grill and the Ulster Bank, which has been in Ranelagh for over 100 years. There is an interesting short terrace of old Georgian houses hidden behind the bank. Other businesses included the Paradise Grill and Digges Medical

Humphreys Pub, 1910. (Courtesy of Humphreys Family)

Hall, whose name has changed but which still operates as a chemist. Pubs have been a strong feature of Ranelagh since the 1850s and despite name changes the old premises continue to serve as pubs. Humphreys Pub at 79 to 81 was established in 1910 and has changed little inside or outside. Smyth's next door from 75 to 77 has been operating since 1900. Birchall's has been dispensing concoctions since 1850.

WOOD FROM THE TREES – BEECHWOOD AND THE NURSERY

Beechwood Avenue marks the boundary between the old villages of Ranelagh and Cullenswood. The original boundary was delineated by the lands of Elm Park House and the extensive Toole's Nursery, an entrance to which was at Mornington Road. This area today stretches from Beechwood Avenue to Anna Villa.

Beechwood Avenue Lower and Upper link the very heart of the residential area of Ranelagh, with their numerous red-brick dwellings, to what is the village of Ranelagh today. These houses date from the 1870s and were built to cater mainly for the clerical classes. For generations before, this was a lane that would have linked those living on the nearby slopes or hills to the village of Cullenswood. The name, like other road names in Ranelagh using words such as 'larch', 'holly' and 'cherry', came from some of the trees grown in Toole's Nurseries, which in itself was shrinking as more and more of its land was taken over for speculative housing, including Beechwood.

THE QUEEN OF TECHNICOLOUR

The famously red-headed Hollywood actress Maureen O'Hara hailed from Beechwood, this time 32 Beechwood Avenue Upper, across the road from the church. She was known for her beauty and for playing fiercely passionate but sensible heroines, often in westerns and adventures. She was reputed to have a very strong chemistry with John Wayne and they starred together in the hugely popular film of the early 1950s, *The Quiet Man*. She became known as the 'Queen of Technicolour' because of her fiery nature, pale skin and vivid red hair. She was born on 17 August 1920 as Maureen Fitzsimons. She was the second oldest of the six children of Charles Stewart Parnell Fitzsimons and Marguerita Lilburn Fitzsimons. Her father was in the clothing business and also bought into Shamrock Rovers Football Club, a team Maureen had supported since childhood. Her mother, a former operatic contralto, was a successful women's clothier. Maureen attended John Street West Girls' School near Thomas Street in Dublin's Liberties and Dominican College on Eccles Street. Her dream at this time was to be a stage actress. She received her early training at a drama school in Rathmines called the Bernadette Players, Richmond Hill, off Mountpleasant Avenue, and at the age of 10 joined the Rathmines Theatre Company and worked in amateur theatre in the evenings, after her lessons.

From the Hunchback to the Quiet Man

She attended a business school and became a proficient bookkeeper and typist. She did well in her Abbey Theatre training and was given an opportunity for a screen test in London. The actor Charles Laughton and his business partner Erich Pommer saw the film clip and offered her an initial seven-year contract with their new company, Mayflower Pictures. Her film career began in the 1930s with her film debut *The Hunchback of Notre Dame* and she later blossomed in such iconic films as *Miracle on 34th Street* and *The Quiet Man*, with John Wayne and Irish actor Barry Fitzgerald. Her name was changed to O'Hara for her role in the Daphne du Maurier-inspired film *Jamaica Inn* (1939). This was her first major film and was directed by Alfred Hitchcock. She moved to the USA when the Second World War began and John Ford cast her as Angharad in *How Green Was My Valley*, which won the 1941 Academy Award for best picture. In 1947, she starred as Doris Walker, the mother of a young Natalie Wood, in *Miracle on 34th Street,* which earned an Academy Award nomination for best picture. In 1946, she became a naturalised citizen of the United States and thereafter held dual US and Irish citizenship.

Maureen was considered one of the world's most beautiful women and is remembered for her onscreen chemistry with John Wayne and the five films they made together: *Rio Grande*, *The Quiet Man*, *The Wings of Eagles*, *McLintock* and *Big Jake*. In 1939, at the age of 19, O'Hara secretly married Englishman George H. Brown, a film producer and scriptwriter whose best-known work is the first of Margaret Rutherford's 1960s Miss Marple mysteries, *Murder She Said*. The marriage was annulled in 1941. Later that year, O'Hara married American film director William Houston Price (dialogue director in *The Hunchback of Notre Dame*), but the union ended in 1953, reportedly as a result of his alcohol abuse. They had one child in 1944, a daughter named Bronwyn Fitzsimons Price.

Ranelagh and the Heart of a Legend

Maureen had homes in Arizona and the Virgin Islands but lived mainly in Glengarriff, County Cork, after suffering a stroke in 2005. In June 2011, she participated at the Maureen O'Hara Film Festival in Glengarriff. The legendary Maureen always regarded Ranelagh with great affection and opened the Ranelagh Arts Festival in 2010. 'Home is where the heart is', she told the audience and reminisced about being from a family of six and having been baptised across the road from her home. She mentioned the Kelly family next door, where there were thirteen children: twelve girls and one boy. The boy later became a priest, Maureen said, 'to protect himself'. She was very generous with her time in Ranelagh on that occasion and of the crowd of over 500, she personally met with at least 200, chatting and signing autographs. She died in 2015 at the age of 95. Terry Connaughton of the festival said, on hearing of her death, 'Maureen was undoubtedly the most famous person ever born in Ranelagh. We believe we are speaking for the community of Ranelagh when we say we are all so proud of her wonderful achievements.'

Maureen's brother, Charles Fitzsimons, is often a forgotten figure in her story, yet he was an important actor and producer in his own right and was also her manager.

MUSICAL EVENINGS IN RANELAGH – KATHLEEN HUGHES AND SEÁN LEMASS

Next door to Maureen O'Hara's house at no. 34 was the home of Kathleen Hughes, who married Seán Lemass, a future Taoiseach. The Lemass and Hughes families knew each other well and used to go on holidays together to Skerries, Co. Dublin. When Seán was in prison, Kathleen used to write to him. The relationship blossomed and they got married in 1924. Her family did not approve of the liaison initially, given his involvement in the War of Independence and politics. Consequently, they used to court

in the back lane behind her home on Upper Beechwood Avenue. She later said that although she knew him for years before they got married, she never dreamt that she would end up marrying him. In earlier years, she studied music with Vincent O'Brien and often sang duets with her father at the musical evenings in Ranelagh, which were so popular at the time. She was always smiling and was famous for her magnificent hats. Together Seán and Kathleen had four children – Maureen (b. 1925), Peggy (1927–2004), Noel (1929–76) and Sheila (1932–97). Maureen married Charles Haughey, minister for justice in Seán Lemass's cabinet, and later Taoiseach. Consequently, both mother and daughter ended up being married to a Taoiseach. Maureen and Charles, having met in UCD, were married in Beechwood Avenue Church in September 1951, the same church Kathleen Hughes and Séan Lemass were married in less than thirty years previously.

FROM THE TWELVE APOSTLES TO 'IS MISE LE MEAS'

Seán Francis Lemass (15 July 1899–11 May 1971) was one of the most prominent Irish politicians of the twentieth century. He served as Taoiseach from 1959 until 1966. Following the Easter Rising, Lemass remained active in the Irish Volunteers, carrying out raids for arms. In November 1920, during the height of the War of Independence, twelve members of the Dublin Brigade of the IRA took part in an attack on British agents living in Dublin, whose names and addresses had been leaked to Collins by his network of spies. The names of those who carried out Collins's orders on the morning of 21 November 1920 were not disclosed until author Tim Pat Coogan mentioned them in his book, *The IRA: A History*, published in 1970. Coogan identified Lemass as a member of 'Apostles' entourage that killed fourteen and wounded five British agents of the Cairo Gang. That day, 21 November 1920, became known as Bloody Sunday after the Black and Tans attacked a Gaelic football game at Croke Park and shot at the innocent crowd and players indiscriminately, killing fourteen civilians. Lemass was arrested in December 1920 and interned at Ballykinlar Camp, County Down.

As a consequence of being a veteran of the 1916 Easter Rising, the War of Independence and the Civil War, Lemass was elected as a Sinn Féin TD for the Dublin South constituency in a by-election on 18 November 1924 and was returned at each election until the constituency was abolished in 1948, when he was re-elected for Dublin South-Central until his retirement in 1969. He was a founder member of Fianna Fáil in 1926, and served as minister for industry and commerce, minister for supplies and Tánaiste in successive Fianna Fáil governments.

The Changing of the Guard

On 23 June 1959, Seán Lemass was appointed Taoiseach on the nomination of Dáil Éireann. Many had wondered if Fianna Fáil could survive without de Valera as leader. However, Lemass quickly established his control of the party. Although he was one of the founding members of Fianna Fáil he was still only 59 years old, 17 years younger than the nearly blind de Valera.

The change of personnel in Fianna Fáil was also accompanied by a change of personnel in Fine Gael, with James Dillon becoming leader upon Richard Mulcahy's retirement in 1959, and in Labour, with Brendan Corish succeeding William Norton in 1960. A generation of leaders who had dominated Irish politics for over three decades had moved off the stage of history – although neither Fine Gael nor Labour's new leaders initiated major policy changes on the level of Lemass's.

Lemass also initiated several changes in the cabinet. He is credited with providing a transitional phase between the old guard and a new generation of professional politicians. Younger men such as Brian Lenihan, Charles Haughey, Patrick Hillery and Michael Hilliard were all given their first cabinet portfolios by Lemass, and ministers who joined under de Valera, such as Jack Lynch, Neil Blaney and Kevin Boland, were promoted by the new Taoiseach. Similarly, several members of the old guard retired from politics during the Lemass era. By 1965, Frank Aiken was the only de Valera veteran remaining in government, and would become the only founder member of Fianna Fáil to survive Lemass as a member of the government and the Dáil.

Rising Tides and a Pound of Tobacco – The Father of Modern Ireland

Lemass summed up his economic philosophy with the oft-quoted phrase, 'A rising tide lifts all boats.' By this he meant that an upsurge in the Irish economy would benefit both the richest and the poorest. Although the White Paper entitled 'Economic Development' was first introduced in 1958 in de Valera's last government, its main recommendations formed the basis for the first programme for economic expansion, which was adopted by Lemass as government policy upon his ascension in 1959. The programme, which was the brainchild of T.K. Whitaker, involved a move away from the protectionist policies that had been in place since the 1930s. Lemass is widely regarded as the father of modern Ireland, primarily due to his efforts in facilitating industrial growth, bringing direct foreign investment into the country, and forging permanent links between Ireland and the European community.

In November 1966, Lemass announced his decision to retire as Fianna Fáil leader and Taoiseach. On 10 November 1966, he officially announced to the Dáil, with his usual penchant for efficiency, 'I have resigned.' He remained a TD until 1969.

During the last few years of his life, Lemass's health began to deteriorate. He had been a heavy pipe smoker all his life, smoking almost a pound of tobacco a week in later life. At the time of his retirement, it was suspected that Lemass had cancer, but this assumption was later disproved. In February 1971, while attending a rugby game at Lansdowne Road, he became unwell; he was rushed to hospital and was told by his doctor that one of his lungs was about to collapse. On Tuesday, 11 May 1971, Seán Lemass died in the Mater Hospital in Dublin, aged 71. He was afforded a state funeral and was buried in Dean's Grange Cemetery.

BIDDY MULLIGAN, THE PRIDE OF THE COOMBE

One of Lemass's former classmates at the O'Connell School and his next-door neighbour on Capel Street was Jimmy O'Dea (1900–65). He was Lemass's best man at his wedding to Kathleen Hughes in the Holy Name Church, Ranelagh, in 1924. In later years, he was to become one of Ireland's best-loved comedians for his inimitable working-class humour, epitomised in such roles as 'Biddy Mulligan, the Pride of the Coombe', a Dublin street vendor.

In the 1920s, O'Dea took part in amateur theatre productions and acted in several early Irish films produced by John MacDonagh. He then met entertainer and writer Harry O'Donovan and together they formed O'D Productions. In the late 1930s, O'D Productions was brought into the Gaiety Theatre by its manager, Louis Elliman, and played there until O'Dea died in January 1965. From 1940 to 1965, O'Dea also continued to tour, most notably in Australia and New Zealand in 1961, and act in films, including Walt Disney's *Darby O'Gill and the Little People* (1959) and the *Rising of the Moon* (1957).

When Jimmy O'Dea married Ursula Doyle, a theatrical impresario, in 1959, Seán Lemass was the best man and the legendary Maureen Potter was the bridesmaid. When O'Dea died in 1965, the Taoiseach, by then Seán Lemass, delivered the graveside oration in Glasnevin Cemetery.

An unusual facet to O'Dea was that although he was small in stature at 5ft4in, he was a giant in Irish, English and Hollywood theatre, film and acting circles. As well as that, he was of the family that made and continue to make some of Ireland's finest mattresses – Odearest Mattresses – 'handmade in Ireland since 1898'. They are the oldest Irish bedmakers still in existence. The business took its name from the O'Dea family, who established manufacturing in Limerick in the late nineteenth century. They expanded quickly and by 1904 had moved to Dublin (Stafford Street and now Wolfe Tone Street), just around the corner from where Jimmy and Seán Lemass grew up together.

THE LION OF THE FOLD AND THE VULTURE OF DARTRY HALL

Two very influential but contrasting individuals lived in the same house on Beechwood Avenue, but at different times. No. 54 Upper Beechwood Avenue was home in *c.* 1924 to the hugely popular Irish labour leader 'Big' Jim (Jem) Larkin (1876–1947), once described as the 'Lion of the fold'. Coincidentally, Douglas Gageby (1918–2004), long-time editor of *The Irish Times*, was born in this house in 1918. Jim Larkin achieved fame and notoriety for his part in leading the infamous 1913 Dublin Lockout, which saw months of strikes in the capital as he led his men in a confrontation with the employers' leader, William Martin Murphy – once described as 'the vulture of Dartry Hall' referring to his palatial Disneyesque residence off Orwell Park, which contrasted the plight of the workers living in squalor in Dublin's tenements.

FROM UNIONIST TO NATIONALIST AND FROM POST OFFICE TO PARLIAMENT

Douglas Gageby was one of the pre-eminent newspaper editors of his generation: he edited the *Evening Press* (1954 onwards) and *The Irish Times* (1963–86). He is credited with having moved the *Times* from being a unionist organ to becoming a successful Irish nationalist newspaper of record. He was involved in controversy from time to time and on one occasion was called a 'white nigger' by Andrew Gilchrist, the British ambassador to Dublin, for his support of the American civil rights movement in the 1960s. His daughter, Susan Denham, is chief justice of the Supreme Court of Ireland.

Not too far from Beechwood Avenue is Mountainview Road, and no. 49 was the home for many years of another prominent leader of the Post Office Workers' Union, William Norton. He was also one-time leader of the Labour Party (1932–60) and a T.D. In the first inter-party government of 1948–51, he became Tánaiste and minister for social welfare and in the second inter-party government (1954–57) minister for industry and commerce. Professor Tom Garvin regarded Norton as pushing 'a modernising agenda' along the lines of that of Seán Lemass.

SURREAL IN RANELAGH – THE JOY OF FANCY FOOTWORK AND KIMONOS

There is not enough space to spell out the sheer quantity and quality of the work and energy of Miriam Gallagher of 53 Upper Beechwood Avenue. She is a playwright, novelist and screenwriter, yet that description is totally inadequate as it does not capture her prolific and endless output of plays, novels and more. The *Sunday Tribune* once commented on 'her inventiveness and style' and her impressive productions were described by the *New York Daily News* as 'vigorous and lively'. Her work has been staged and screened in Ireland, Europe, Australia, the USA, Canada, and South Africa, with Irish, Dutch, French, Finnish and Russian translations.

Her published plays include: *Fancy Footwork* (1997); *Kalahari Blues* (2006 – three plays); *The Gold of Tradaree* (2008 – three plays) and *Green Rain – Irish Composers on Stage* (2011). Her fiction includes *Pusakis at Paros* (2008) and *Song for Salamander* (2004), launched at the United Arts Club, Dublin, by Macdara Woods, a leading Irish poet and Ranelagh resident, who called it 'A paradigm for our times'. Her film *Gypsies* has been screened in Ireland, the UK, New York, San Francisco and at the International Children's Film Festival, Hyderabad, India. She received Arts Council and European Script Fund awards for *Girls in Silk Kimonos* (a feature-length screenplay celebrating Constance and Eva Gore Booth). *The Parting Glass* and *Doracha Mór agus Seoltóirí Ghaoth Dobhair* won national and international awards. According to *The Irish Times*, 'she shows vivid imagination and is something of a surrealist' and the *Evening Herald* noted that she 'combines the real with the surreal'. *Fancy Footwork* (Dublin Theatre Festival) was performed by Mountjoy prisoners at Focus

Theatre, Dublin. It was a unique occasion as it was the only time in the history of the state that prisoners were released to perform in a professional theatre.

THE FIRST JEWISH LORD MAYOR OF DUBLIN

The Briscoe political dynasty started at no. 21 Beechwood Avenue, the home of Robert Briscoe (1894–1969), the son of a Lithuanian Jewish refugee. His father had come to Ireland penniless but had subsequently prospered through hard work and a charming personality. For many years, he had a furniture business on Ormond Quay called Lawlor Briscoe. Robert had fought in the War of Independence, went to America with Éamon de Valera and following the Civil War became a TD for thirty-eight years. He had also been a key figure in the formation of the Fianna Fáil party. He became the first Jewish Lord Mayor of Dublin in 1956. His son, Ben Briscoe, also served as Lord Mayor of Dublin in 1988/89.

THE SINGING FLAMES AND THE FITZGERALD'S

Further up the road is no. 51, which was once a 'safe house' used by Volunteers during the War of Independence. It was the family home of Seamus Moore, who later became a Fianna Fáil TD. Among those who hid out in this house was Ernie O'Malley, who had just escaped from Kilmainham Jail and who later wrote about his exploits in *On Another Man's Wound* and *The Singing Flame*. When O'Malley arrived at the house he encountered another man on the run – Desmond FitzGerald, future government minister and father of Garret FitzGerald, future Taoiseach.

FROM THE QUIET MAN TO OLD GOBBO

In Ranelagh there is no escaping the Maureen O'Hara influence and connection. Jack MacGowran, the great Beckett interpreter and Victor MacLagen's sidekick in *The Quiet Man*, grew up on 46 Lower Beechwood Avenue and spent forty years of his life living in the village. He was a character actor probably best known for his work with Samuel

Beckett. He was a frail-looking, bird-like man, whose frame and sharp features belied his power and talent. Born John Joseph MacGowran (1918–73), he started work as an insurance salesman and part-time actor. He began his full-time acting career in the Abbey Theatre, was a comical figure on and off stage and later achieved stage renown for his interpretations of the works of Beckett. He appeared as Lucky in *Waiting for Godot* at the Royal Court Theatre, and with the Royal Shakespeare Company in *Endgame*. He also specialised in the works of Seán O'Casey. While with the Royal Shakespeare Company, he became great friends with Peter O'Toole. While working with that group, he once played Old Gobbo *The Merchant of Venice*. When the scenery arrived, the director called the cast to view the set. MacGowran did not appear with the rest of the cast and when the director queried this a messenger conveyed a message to him: 'Mr MacGowran says that if you had read the play you would know that Old Gobbo was blind.'

He acted in a number of films with an Irish theme, including *No Resting Place* (1951), *The Quiet Man* (when he played Aloysius Feeney, the pallid yes-man to Red Will Danagher), *The Gentle Gunman* (1952), *Rooney* (1958) and *Darby O'Gill and the Little People* (1959). His last film was *The Exorcist* (1973).

ANNA VILLA AND GARRET THE GOOD

Not only does Garret FitzGerald, who was Taoiseach twice in the 1980s, have links with Beechwood Avenue, but he spent his last years on a nearby road, Anna Villa. He stayed with his son and family. Prior to that move, he had been living on nearby Palmerston Road, Rathmines. He was affectionately known as 'Garrett the good' as it was recognised that he wanted, first and foremost, to serve the people of Ireland selflessly, without fear or favour. It was said of him that he was an original and there were no copies or prints.

Anna Villa is just off the main Ranelagh thoroughfare as it weaves its way through the two villages. The junction would have been the centre of the old Cullenswood Village. This is a narrow winding road containing higgledy-piggledy dwellings of all shapes and sizes, with some dating back to the eighteenth century. It was originally a lane linking Milltown Path to the village of Cullenswood. Then it was called Anne Street as it provided a connection for a house called Anna Villa to the village. Later on, it was extended to connect with Palmerston Road and Upper Cross/Upper Rathmines.

Amongst the many eclectic houses, no. 20 is a striking three-storey dwelling with a cottage on each side giving an attractive and distinctive appearance to this part of the road. Many of the older houses on this side of the road have other interesting features, such as ornamental fanlights.

FIRST BIKE IN RANELAGH FOR TOUR DE FRANCE WINNER

Anna Villa was the first home of the famous and foremost Irish cyclist and Tour de France winner Stephen Roche. In 1987, his finest year, he became the world's no. 1 cyclist upon winning the triple crown, having had major successes in the Giro d'Italia, the Tour de France (his dream win) and the World Championship in Austria. He became the first sportsman to win the Freedom of the City of Dublin. He retired in 1993 with fifty-eight professional wins to his name. He was aged 3 or 4 when he got his first bike, which was a small blue second-hand children's bike bought in Ranelagh.

THE FRENCH CONNECTION AND IRELAND

Between Beechwood Avenue and Anna Villa is Ashfield Road and just off that is Ashfield Avenue. This was the home (no. 13) of renowned photographer Robert French. His photographic legacy lives on today in the Lawrence Collection of late-nineteenth- and early-twentieth-century images held in the National Library of Ireland. Lawrence himself was not a photographer but he employed French as his chief photographer. Lawrence had his photographic studio on Sackville Street (now O'Connell Street), opposite the GPO. This was originally his mother's toy and fancy goods shop, but Lawrence was somewhat of an entrepreneur. French was born in Dublin and spent some time working in the Royal Irish Constabulary (RIC). He then joined Lawrence's studio and worked his way up as a printer, artist and then assistant photographer. He took over 30,000 of the photographs in the Lawrence Collection. The collection consists of 40,000 glass plates mainly from the period 1880 to 1914. Lawrence's business prospered for nearly fifty years. French retired in 1914. Over the years, French photographed the length and breadth of

Ireland, from Howth Head in the east to Achill Head in the west and from Malin Head in the north to Skibbereen in the south. This unique visual collection captures Irish life in many of its aspects in the late nineteenth and early twentieth centuries. The glass plates were acquired by the National Library shortly after the firm closed down in 1942.

Just off Ashfield Avenue was an old 'slaughter house' or abattoir, which catered for the many butcher shops in the vicinity.

EDENVALE ROAD AND THE IRISH LITERARY REVIVAL

Edenvale Road, near Anna Villa, was originally part of the infamous Bloody Fields that stretched over to present-day Palmerston Park, site of one of the most pivotal battles in Irish history – the Battle of Rathmines in 1649. Padraic Colum (1881–1972), poet, playwright, children's author, novelist, collector of folklore, and a leading member of the Irish Literary Revival, was probably one of its most eminent residents, staying every year in his sister's house at no. 11. His wife Mary used to teach nearby in St Ita's School on Oakley Road (Cullenswood Avenue). He wrote some sixty books, not counting his plays. Some of his most famous poems include 'She Moves through the Fair' and 'The Drover'. He worked with W.B. Yeats, Lady Gregory and George Russell and was a member of the first board of the Abbey Theatre. However, he fell out with Yeats over the staging of Synge's *Playboy of the Western World*. He was a lifelong friend of James Joyce. Colum had also lived at no. 30 Chelmsford Avenue and at 22 Killeen Road, both in Ranelagh, at different stages of his life.

FROM ARTHUR GUINNESS TO STEPTOE & SON

Another famous resident of Edenvale Road, who was born at no. 6, was the actor who made the English television comedy soap *Steptoe and Son* (1962–74) hugely popular. His name was Henry Wilfred Brambell (1912–85) and his father worked in the Guinness brewery. Brambell junior worked part-time with *The Irish Times* and at the Abbey Theatre after leaving school. He turned professional at the Gate Theatre. It was his ability to play old men, including Dickens's

Scrooge, that led to him being cast as Albert Steptoe, probably his best-remembered role. He played the cantankerous father of Harry Corbett, who was a rag-and-bone merchant. Many scenes are still remembered, including him marching around with the horse and cart, collecting rags and every conceivable kind of junk, or Wilfred eating pickled onions while taking a bath.

DIONYSIUS AND BOUCICAULT

Sallymount is an old part of Ranelagh and is shown on an 1837 map of the area. It starts at the Bank of Ireland on Sandford Road and leads down to Appian Way and Leeson Park. It was laid out in 1770 and is regarded as one of the oldest terraces in Dublin. Walter Thomas Meyler lived here from the 1820s. He was later involved in the Young Ireland movement and became editor of the *Irish Tribune*. Dionysius Lardner, father of the famous Dion Boucicault, actor and dramatist, also lived here. Patrick and Willie Pearse spent some time residing here in a house called Brookville, near the end of Chelmsford Lane. Long after their departure to Cullenswood and then to Rathfarnham, and the 1916 Rising, the house was abandoned, forgotten and allowed to crumble.

THE BARON, COLLIER'S AND WONG'S

Beyond the old villages of Ranelagh and Cullenswood, and past Anna Villa and the early-nineteenth-century whitewashed cottages on Collier's Avenue (previously known as Major's Lane after the notorious Major Sirr), Sandford Road begins and leads towards Milltown, Clonskeagh, Donnybrook and beyond. The name 'Sandford' came from George Sandford, 3rd Baron of Sandford (George, Baron Mount Sandford), who lived in Sandford Park House (now part of the school), near what was to become Sandford Parish Church, of which he was the benefactor.

The corner of Collier's Avenue, where Wong's Chinese restaurant was until recently, was once the location of the famous Sandford cinema. Generations of local children queued in the lane waiting to gain admittance. Inside they might be terrorised by the power-mad uniformed usher flashing his torch this way and every way and woe betide you if he took a dislike to you!

MERTON HOUSE AND THE BIRTH OF A NATION

Nearby was Merton House, which later gave its name to some of the roads in the immediate vicinity. This was the residence of Robert Newenham. Later, the Young Irelander Charles Gavan Duffy (1816–9 February 1903) lived there for a time until his arrest and transportation to Australia in 1847. There he became prime minister of Victoria. A very able man, this Irish nationalist, journalist, poet and finally Australian politician was the eighth premier of Victoria and one of the most colourful figures in Irish and Australian political history. Duffy was born in Dublin Street, Monaghan town, the son of a Catholic shopkeeper. Both his parents died while he was still a child and his uncle, Fr James Duffy, who was the Catholic parish priest of Castleblayney, became his guardian for a number of years. He was educated at St Malachy's College in Belfast and was admitted to the Irish Bar in 1845. Even before being admitted to the Bar, Duffy was active on the Irish land question. He also became a leading figure in Irish literary circles. He edited *Ballad Poetry of Ireland* (1843) and other works on Irish literature. Gavan Duffy was one of the founders of *The Nation* and became its first editor; the two others were Thomas Osborne Davis and John Blake Dillon, who would later become Young Irelanders. All three were members of Daniel O'Connell's Repeal Association. *The Nation*, under Gavan Duffy, transformed from a literary voice into a 'rebellious organisation'.

FROM MONSTER MEETINGS TO PARIS

As a result of *The Nation*'s support for repeal, Gavan Duffy, as owner, was arrested and convicted of seditious conspiracy in relation to the monster meeting planned for Clontarf, just outside Dublin, but was released after an appeal to the House of Lords. In August 1850, he formed the Tenant Right League to bring about reforms in the Irish land system and protect tenants' rights, and in 1852 he was elected to the House of Commons for New Ross. In November 1852, Lord Derby's government introduced a land bill to secure for evicted Irish tenants, in accordance with the principles of the Tenant League, compensation for improvements, prospective and retrospective, made by them on the land. The bill passed the House of Commons in 1853 and 1854, but in both years failed to pass the House of Lords.

In 1855 the cause of the Irish tenants, and indeed of Ireland generally, seemed to Duffy more hopeless than ever. Broken in health and spirit, he published in 1855 a farewell address to his constituency, declaring that he had resolved to retire from parliament, as it was no longer possible to accomplish the task for which he had solicited their votes. In 1856, despairing of the prospects for Irish independence, he resigned from the House of Commons and emigrated with his family to Australia. After being feted in Sydney and Melbourne, Duffy settled in the newly formed colony of Victoria. Following a successful, though not easy, career in Australian politics, Duffy eventually retired to the south of France in 1880, where he continued to support the Irish Home Rule struggle.

THE DUFFY DYNASTY AND ROGER CASEMENT'S TRIAL

Duffy married for a third time in Paris in 1881, to Louise Hall, and had four more children in his seventies. One of his sons by a previous marriage was John Gavan Duffy, a Victorian politician between 1874 and 1904. Another son, Sir Frank Gavan Duffy, was chief justice of the High Court of Australia from 1931 to 1935. His daughter, Louise, was an Irish republican present at the 1916 Easter Rising. She was an Irish-language enthusiast who founded an Irish-language school for girls in Dublin – at Cullenswood Avenue, Ranelagh. Yet another son, Mr Justice George Gavan Duffy (born 1882), was an Irish politician and later (from 1936) a judge of the Irish High Court, becoming its president from 1946 until his death in 1951. In 1916 it was he who defended Roger Casement at his trial for treason in London. A grandson, Charles Leonard Gavan Duffy, was a judge on the Supreme Court of Victoria, Australia.

MONEY, MUSIC AND PEAT BRIQUETTES

Ranelagh is replete with different architectural styles dating from the late eighteenth century right up to the twenty-first century. Between Collier's Avenue, with its line of old cottages, and Sandford Park Church, is an interesting terrace of mock-Tudor houses dating from the early twentieth century. The residents were as interesting as their dwellings. Number 27 was the home of Michele Esposito, an Italian musician who became professor of music in the Royal Irish Academy of Music for most of the first half of the twentieth century. He was also the founder of the Dublin Orchestral Society. Number 11 was the home of Ernest Blythe, the Irish Free State's finance minister in the 1920s and later director of the Abbey Theatre. A Latvian national, Janis Mezs, who lived in no. 6, had an influence on the development growth of the Irish Shipping Company during the Emergency and helped Bord na Móna master the process of making briquettes.

THE PRESIDENT, THE COMMISSIONER AND THE COFFEE CUP

Just beyond the church at no. 45 Sandford Terrace was the internationally renowned Dillon Garden, which was often open for viewing for nigh on twenty years until 2015. It sold for €4.5 million when the Dillons retired from gardening. Former President of Ireland and later UN High Commissioner Mary Robinson lived next door. Prior to taking office in Áras an Uachtaráin in 1990, Robinson and her family lived in this fine detached Georgian property on Sandford Terrace.

Robinson has had a fascinating career, full of achievements and accolades. Mary Therese Winifred Robinson (b. 1944) served as the seventh – and first female – President of Ireland from 1990 to 1997, and then as the United Nations high commissioner for human rights from 1997 to 2002. She first rose to prominence as an academic, barrister, campaigner and member of the Irish Senate (1969–89). She defeated Fianna Fáil's Brian Lenihan and Fine Gael's Austin Currie in the 1990 presidential election.

Human Rights Advocate Par Excellence

Robinson is widely regarded as a transformative figure for Ireland, and for the Irish presidency, revitalising and liberalising a previously conservative, low-profile political office. During her UN tenure, she visited Tibet (1998), the first high commissioner to do so; she criticised Ireland's immigrant policy; and she criticised the use of capital punishment in the United States. She extended her intended single four-year term by a year to preside over the World Conference against Racism 2001 in Durban, South Africa.

After leaving the UN in 2002, Robinson formed Realizing Rights: The Ethical Globalization Initiative. Its core activities were 1) fostering equitable trade and decent work, 2) promoting the right to health and more humane migration policies, and 3) working to strengthen women's leadership and encourage corporate social responsibility.

Robinson returned to live in Ireland at the end of 2010, and has set up the Mary Robinson Foundation – Climate Justice, which aims to be 'a centre for thought leadership, education and advocacy on the struggle to secure global justice for those many victims of climate change who are usually forgotten – the poor, the disempowered and the marginalised across the world'.

Robinson is chair of the Institute for Human Rights and Business and chancellor of the University of Dublin. Since 2004, she has also been professor of practice in international affairs at Columbia University, where she teaches international human rights. She is also chair of the International Institute for Environment and Development (IIED) and is a founding member and chair of the Council of Women World Leaders. In 2004 she received Amnesty International's Ambassador of Conscience Award for her work in promoting human rights.

A few doors from the Dillons and Robinsons, Joseph Bewley of the Bewley coffee empire lived at no. 1 Sandford Terrace. The Bewleys lived in different houses in the area until 1950 and one such residence, Sandford Hill, later became part of the nearby Gonzaga College. The Bewley family also had a fine house in Rathgar. This impressive house (on the site of the present-day high school), was originally on 30 acres of farmland and was built in 1906 by Ernest Bewley, proprietor of the famous Bewley's Oriental Café on Grafton and Westmoreland streets, who was the first occupant. It was divided into Danum Meadows and Danum Firs in the early 1940s. It remained in the Bewley family until the Gonzaga College acquired it in the 1960s. It now covers 22 acres. Ernest Bewley started his business ventures in Dublin with a modest coffee shop in the late nineteenth century. The Bewley family were Quakers who originated in France and moved to Ireland in the eighteenth century. They entered the tea trade and in 1835 Samuel Bewley and his son landed an unprecedented cargo of 2,099 chests of tea, shipped directly from China to Dublin, thereby breaking the East India Tea Company's monopoly. The Bewley family subsequently

expanded into the coffee trade and in the late nineteenth century they opened cafés on George's Street (1894) and Westmoreland Street (1896) in Dublin. The Grafton Street landmark branch opened in 1927 and became one of Dublin's most popular institutions.

FROM THE DUKE OF WELLINGTON TO TUTANKHAMUN'S TOMB

The Bewley's building on Grafton Street had once housed Whyte's Academy, a school whose pupils included the Duke of Wellington and Robert Emmet. Ernest Bewley undertook a complete refurbishment of the building, drawing inspiration from the great European cafés of Paris and Vienna, as well as exotic oriental tearooms and Egyptian architecture (the façade was inspired by the discovery of Tutankhamun's tomb in 1922). The centrepiece of the café remains to this day the six magnificent stained-glass windows commissioned from the renowned artist Harry Clarke, who completed them just prior to his death in 1931. The grandeur and ambition of Ernest Bewley's achievement resulted in Bewley's on Grafton Street becoming an essential part of the literary, cultural, artistic, architectural and social life of Dublin. The flagship café became a haunt for some of Ireland's most famous literary and artistic figures, including James Joyce (who mentioned the café in his book *Dubliners*), Patrick Kavanagh, Samuel Beckett and Seán O'Casey.

CHERRIES AND HOLLY – HOMESICK AT *THE NEW YORKER*

Two adjacent roads with similar architecture but contrasting styles stand out just off Sandford Road, beyond Sandford Terrace – Cherryfield Avenue and Hollybank Road. The former is distinctive for its width and brightness, with the exterior front walls of nearly every house completely painted in bright blue, whites or grey pastel shades. This creates a bright and somewhat startling effect in an area filled with darker red bricks, including Hollybank Avenue, which runs parallel to it. The latter road, before it was developed from 1906 onwards, was known as 'Baron George's fields' as it was where the young George Sandford played as a child.

Cherryfield Avenue was built subsequently and it was at no. 48 Cherryfield Avenue that Maeve Brennan (1917–93), short-story writer and long-time journalist with *The New Yorker* magazine, was reared before moving to New York where she became a writer. Her father, a strong Irish republican, had been appointed the Irish Free State's representative in the USA. After Maeve was born in Great Denmark Street, her family moved to Belgrave Road and then Cherryfield

Avenue in 1921. In 1934 she moved to New York with her family. A few years later, after a spell of working for *Harper's Bazaar,* she began the connection with *The New Yorker* magazine which continued until her death. She was widely read in the USA, but virtually unknown in Ireland. The Ranelagh area and her terraced house are the settings for almost half of her forty short stories. These communicate authentic representations of the fear and anxiety that can permeate modern life. Themes of repression, masquerades, hope, dreams, frustration, loneliness, despair and brittle relationships in post-independence Ireland fill her stories. Her parents were both active in the War of Independence, a theme also reflected in her stories.

The Long-Winded Lady and Springs of Affection

Maeve Brennan was admired for her intelligence, beauty, wit and style. She was a petite woman who liked dressing in black and frequently wore large dark glasses. During her life-time she was perhaps best known for her column 'The Long-Winded Lady', which she wrote for the New Yorker from 1954 to 81, but since her death there has been a new appreciation of her stories and the subtlety and sharpness of her sometimes acerbic powers of observation. A collection of her short stories, *The Springs of Affection*, and a novella, *The Visitor,* were re-issued in the late 1990s. She was also celebrated by another resident of Cherryfield Avenue, the academic Angela Bourke, who wrote a biography of Maeve Brennan, *Homesick at the New Yorker.*

From the Feis Ceoil to Philadelphia

By an extraordinary coincidence Brennan's Ranelagh home was also the house that actor Eamon Morrissey was reared in. Years later he recalled how the hairs on the back of his neck stood up when he read a story by Maeve Brennan in the *New Yorker* and discovered that both had called no. 48 'home'. He discovered this travelling on the subway while performing in New York. Eamon later wrote a play called *Maeve's House.* He was an only child, and his father bought the house in 1934 when the Brennans moved to Washington. By another coincidence, Eamon's mother was also called Maeve. Eamon recalled that when he was growing up, Ranelagh was like a country village full of all kinds of shops. There was no going into the city for supplies. Even the hardware shop had a sign that stated 'goods at city prices'.

His parents encouraged his early interest in stage performance and he won several medals for his recitations at the Feis Ceoil. While still in his teens and a pupil at Synge Street CBS, Morrissey worked part-time as a stage manager in various Dublin theatres. He left school before sitting the Leaving Certificate in order to try his hand at acting in London. After spending several years there doing odd jobs, he was chosen for the part of Ned, the emigrant, in the 1964 world première of Brian Friel's *Philadelphia, Here I Come!*

The Brother and Hall's Pictorial Weekly

Friel's play later became a huge success on Broadway and Morrissey enjoyed a lengthy sojourn in the United States as a member of the cast. In July 1967, another Friel play, *Lovers*, opened at the Gate Theatre in Dublin with Morrissey in the leading role of Joe.

In 1974, Morrissey adapted the satirical writings of Brian O'Nolan (Flann O'Brien/Myles na gCopaleen) into a successful one-man show entitled *The Brother*. In his two-hour solo performance, Morrissey portrayed a porter-swilling, nose-picking pub philosopher with ingenious solutions to the world's problems. Morrissey went on to create two more one-man shows, *Patrick Gulliver*, drawn from the works of Jonathan Swift, and *Joycemen*, which features various characters from James Joyce's *Ulysses*.

In 1977, Morrissey won a Jacob's Award for his performances in Frank Hall's long-running satirical TV series *Hall's Pictorial Weekly*. Each week he appeared as a variety of grotesque characters, most notably the minister for hardship (based on the then minister Richie Ryan aka 'Richie Ruin').

FROM COLDBLOW HOUSE TO THE CONSTITUTION OF IRELAND

Continuing along Sandford Road, across from the entrance to present-day Milltown Park is Belmont Avenue, previously called Coldblow Lane. This linked Donnybrook Village to the fine house owned by Sir William Fortick, called Coldblow House and Demesnes (now Milltown Park). A subsequent owner was Denis George, recorder of Dublin and a baron of the exchequer. The lands around the demesne were known for generations as 'Baron George's Fields'. Coldblow Lane was named after the local landowner Colonel Coldblow.

In 1858 the Jesuits bought the house and land and opened a small retreat house and two years later a novitiate with thirty students. Since then the Jesuits have had a strong presence in Ranelagh, including the secondary school for boys, Gonzaga College, and the Jesuit Training College, which evolved into the Milltown Institute of Theology and Philosophy. The National College of Industrial Relations was also founded by the Jesuits (Fr Edward Joseph Coyne, in particular) on its lands at Milltown Park. Fr Edward (Ned) Joseph Coyne SJ (1896–1958) was also an economist and sociologist and served as its principal from 1951 to 1954. Coyne was professor of moral theology in Milltown. He served on a number of government commissions and other organisations. He was chairman of the Irish Agricultural Organisation Society. While formulating the 1937 Irish Constitution, Éamon de Valera was advised by Fr Coyne, among others.

BIRTH OF A CONSTITUTION – CAHILL, COYNE AND THE 1937 CONSTITUTION

Besides Fr Coyne, a number of other Jesuit priests, based at Milltown Park, had an influence on the drafting of the 1937 Constitution of Ireland and a number of articles in it reflect this. They had been invited by Éamon de Valera to make submissions containing their views on what should or should not be included. The document was created over a period of three years, formally beginning with the meeting of a civil service committee in May 1934 to review the 1922 Constitution. Subsequently, in September 1936, de Valera requested and received a document called 'Suggestions for a Catholic Constitution' from the Jesuit order (Frs Patrick Bartley, John McErlean, Joseph Canavan and Edward Coyne) at Milltown Park. There was also Fr Edward Cahill's 'Supplementary Suggestions'. From this point through to the Constitution's adoption, de Valera also corresponded with John Charles McQuaid, the Holy Ghost priest based in Blackrock College who a few years later became Archbishop of Dublin. His influence on many aspects of the document was pronounced, according to certain scholars. However, the competing strands, personalities, organisations and publications of the time all showed that on the eve of the publication of the Draft Constitution there was a diversity of currents and opinion in Irish Catholicism which would have made its writing more difficult than might first have been thought.

DE VALERA AND CAHILL'S 'SPECIAL POSITION' CLAUSE

An indication of these strains and currents is the case of Fr Edward Cahill, also based in Milltown Park. Fr Edward Cahill differed with his confreres, and they most certainly differed with him, to the point of trying to sideline him from the serious deliberations. Well known and vociferous, Cahill was in good company with other opinion leaders of the Catholic Action Movement in the 1930s which included Fr Denis Fahey, Fr John Charles McQuaid and Alfred O'Rahilly. Cahill had sent de Valera a copy of his huge volume, *The Framework of a Christian State*, and de Valera replied thanking him and saying, 'It is worth reading and re-reading, and I believe it will be consulted for advice and guidance in the years ahead'. Following this, in September 1936, Cahill wrote to de Valera enclosing a long submission for a new constitution. De Valera found Cahill's contribution as 'useful as indicating the principles which should inspire all governmental activity so as to make it conform to Catholic teaching'. He also suggested that Cahill draw up draft articles and a draft preamble 'and when I have seen your draft, to have a chat with you about it'. Following this the above-mentioned Jesuit subcommittee that included Cahill was formed. The final Constitution displayed very much the same principles as the Jesuit submission. Cahill followed that submission with additional suggestions and he changed the Jesuit committee's word 'preponderant' to 'special position' in relation to wording surrounding the Catholic Church's position and inclusion in the Constitution. It would appear then that both the main Jesuit submission and Cahill's additions influenced de Valera's deliberations, if not directly, then certainly indirectly.

A TITANIC ACHIEVEMENT – FROM THE EYE OF THE STORM TO IRELAND'S EYE

By an extraordinary coincidence two of the most famous photographers in Ireland in the nineteenth and twentieth centuries, Robert French (the Lawrence Collection in the National Library of Ireland) and Fr Francis Browne SJ, who lived with his Jesuit community in Milltown Park, were based in Ranelagh.

By the time of his death in 1960, Fr Browne had accumulated a collection of more than 40,000 negatives. However, these were virtually forgotten until a Fr Edward O'Donnell, twenty-five years later, happened to discover them, including photographs, in an old black metal trunk in a basement of the Jesuit provincial house in Milltown Park.

Most amazingly of all, in this collection was an album containing photographs of the *Titanic*'s last fatal voyage. By the time of Fr O'Donnell's discovery, Fr Browne had been almost forgotten, but investigations revealed he had enjoyed fame in 1912 when images of the *Titanic*'s journey to Cobh were published in newspapers worldwide. He had travelled first class to Cobh, having been given a ticket by his uncle, Robert Browne, Bishop of Cloyne. His remarkable pictures proved to be unique.

Ypres, the Somme and the Most Decorated Chaplain

Fr Browne's introduction to photography began in 1897 when his uncle gave him his first camera, prior to him going on a Grand Tour of Europe. He honed his skills on this tour. Year later, he was made a chaplain during the First World War, and saw action at Ypres and on the Somme. He became the most decorated chaplain during the war. After the war, he returned to his teaching duties in Belvedere College and elsewhere, yet retained his interest in photography. Most of his collection documents an emerging Ireland in the decades following the War of Independence. He was described by one critic as 'a master photographer with an unerring eye'.

Since Fr O'Donnell's discovery in 1985, Fr Browne's photographs have been published in book form and exhibited around the world. He is now recognised, not only as the greatest photographer in Ireland in the first half of the twentieth century, but as an outstanding photographer of world stature.

FROM BIRD-STUFFER TO NOVELIST
– WILLIAM CARLETON

Just across the road from the entrance to Milltown Park, at the corner of Sandford Road and Belmont Avenue, is an old detached dwelling called Woodville. William Carleton (1794–1869), lived out the last years of his life in this house. Carleton was a popular nineteenth-century novelist and writer, who spent most of his working life in Dublin. He was best known for his *Traits and Stories of the Irish Peasantry* (1830), a collection of ethnic sketches of the stereotypical Irishman. Born in Co. Tyrone, Carleton's father was a Catholic tenant farmer who supported fourteen children on as many acres, and young Carleton passed his early life among scenes similar to those he later described in his books. He was steeped in folklore from an early age. His father, who had an extraordinary memory (he knew the Bible by heart) and was a native Irish speaker, had a thorough acquaintance with Irish folklore, and told stories by the fireside. His mother, a noted singer, sang in the Irish language. Carleton received a basic education. As his father moved from one small farm to another, he attended various 'hedge' (outdoor) schools, which used to be a notable feature of Irish life. A picture of one of these schools occurs in the sketch called 'The Hedge School' included in *Traits and Stories of the Irish Peasantry*.

Phil Purcell the Pig Driver

Carleton was an unlikely candidate to become a best-selling novelist in Victorian England and Ireland. In 1819 he came to Dublin with 2 shillings and sixpence in his pocket in the hope of finding fame and fortune. Carleton began his working life seeking a job as a bird-stuffer. However, his proposal to use potatoes and meal as stuffing failed to impress his prospective employer. He then tried to become a soldier, but the colonel of the regiment dissuaded him – Carleton had applied in Latin. After staying in a number of cheap lodgings, he eventually found a place in a house in the Liberties, on Francis Street, which contained a circulating library. The landlady allowed him to read from twelve to sixteen hours a day. In 1830 he published his first full-length book, *Traits and Stories of the Irish Peasantry* (two volumes), which made his name and is considered among his best achievements. In it he stereotyped the Irish 'Paddy' in sketches such as 'Phil Purcell the Pig Driver'. He was, in his own words, the 'historian of their habits and manners, their feelings, their prejudices, their superstitions and their crimes' (preface to *Tales of Ireland*). His novel of the famine, *The Black Prophet*, is seen by many as the high point of his work, as in later years he sacrificed quality to quantity in an attempt to alleviate his numerous debts. He died in 1869 and is buried in Mount Jerome Cemetery.

Carleton's work is considered important for his insider knowledge of the peasant life of Ireland, though he has been criticised for playing to the gallery in his sometimes stereotypical stage Irish characters.

THE QUEEN AND THE ROYAL PENNY

First appearances give one a cosy and comfortable impression of the fine, ivy-covered, detached country home Belmont House, hidden away a few hundred metres from the heart of Ranelagh Village. Facing the side entrance to Woodville on Belmont Avenue is this elegant two-storey, four rooms upstairs and four downstairs, Georgian house. This is one of Dublin's oldest houses and was once visited by Queen Victoria. Immediately adjacent, at the Ranelagh end of Belmont Avenue, are a few other older dwellings from a bygone era. The house dates from *c*. 1760 when Belmont Avenue was called Coldblow Lane. Belmont House was originally part of the Milltown Park Estate, but was separated from the property, being just 100 metres away from the main entrance, when the Jesuits bought the estate in 1858. Some local people suggest that Belmont House was originally a dower house or a house for a mistress of one of the owners of the estate. Other views suggest that it was a coach house and there is some evidence of this from old maps.

An interesting story attached to the house relates to Queen Victoria's visit to Ireland in 1849. While journeying along the main Sandford Road travelling toward Clonskeagh and beyond, to Mount Anville and the home of William Dargan, the great engineer and pioneer of Irish rail, she was caught short. Where else to go then but to nearby Belmont House to spend a royal penny. In more recent times an owner of the houses, Tom St John, owned a number of well-known cinemas in the heart of Dublin – the Capitol, the Regent, the Ambassador and the Academy. His wife, Maeve, had family links to the Kennedy Bakery business.

4

FROM THE HEART OF THE REVOLUTION TO DUNVILLE VILLAGE

THE TOWNSHIP AND OAKLEY

Retracing our steps back to the heart of Ranelagh, at the junction of Beechwood Avenue and Dunville Avenue, we have one end of Oakley Road that begins or ends at the Triangle. At the Triangle junction, also, Charleston Road begins and leads to Belgrave Square, Castlewood Avenue and the rest of Rathmines.

Oakley Road was formerly known as Dunville Lane, then Cullenswood Avenue and later still, in the 1890s, Oakley Road, deriving its name from Oakley House. The township administrators did not want to have any mention of the Gaelic-derived name, Cullenswood, in Ranelagh. To confuse matters even further, the road sign for Oakley Road today has a supposed Irish version – Bóthar Feadha Cuileann, which sounds more like an Irish version of Cullenswood rather than Oakley!

SCHOOLS AND SCHOLARS

Midwifery and the Murder Machine
At the Dunville Avenue end of this narrow and winding picturesque road is Cullenswood House, a property steeped in scholarship and history. It was associated with William Joly in the early nineteenth century, and was subsequently the childhood home of well-known historian William Lecky. It also has a connection to Bartholomew Mosse, surgeon and founder of the Rotunda Lying-In Hospital, who

died in 1759. He had developed an interest in midwifery while working in hospitals around Europe and in Paris in particular. His successor at the hospital was Fielding Ould.

The house was later bought by Pádraig Pearse to establish his first Irish-language school, St Enda's, in 1908. He once described the house as 'one of the noble old Georgian mansions'. His opinion of the Irish education system at the time is best summed up in the phrase 'murder machine'. His alternative system of education was built on the principle of giving the pupils 'freedom' to develop as persons. Part of his curriculum placed an emphasis on the importance of drama. Near the entrance to the school, beneath a fresco of Cuchulainn, he had written his philosophy, 'I care not if I live one day and one night if only my fame and deeds live after me'. He is now best known for his role as the leader of the 1916 Rising. Pearse was executed in Kilmainham Jail in May 1916.

From St Enda's to Lios na nÓg

Republican, educationalist and writer Pádraig Pearse had a brief but significant connection with the Ranelagh district. In 1910 his school moved to larger premises in Rathfarnham, and Cullenswood became the location for an Irish-language girl's school, St Ita's, until 1912. It played an active role in the War of Independence, acting as a 'safe house'. Michael Collins also used a hidden cellar in the basement of the house as an office. The house was raided and destroyed by the Black and Tans. It was subsequently repaired and in 1960 Margaret Pearse, sister of Pádraig Pearse, sold it to the state. Today the tradition of bilingual education is continuing with Scoil Bhríde and Gaelscoil Lios na nÓg. More than 100 years after Pearse's dream for the house, it continues to keep his hope for Ireland very much alive – 'a country without its own language is only half a country'.

The Gifford Sisters, Biscuits and Pianos

Oakley Road was also home to some of the other signatories of the 1916 Proclamation of Independence, including Thomas MacDonagh, who taught as St Enda's from 1908. After their marriage in the Church of the Holy Name, Beechwood Avenue, he and his new wife, Muriel (*née* Gifford, one of the famous Gifford sisters) lived in no. 29 Oakley Road. Their children Donagh and Bairbre were born in that house. He was a poet, founder of *The Irish Review*, involved in literary circles and a founder of the Irish Volunteers. He was also involved in the Howth gun-running episode of 1914 when hundreds of rifles were smuggled into Ireland. He was on the Military Council for the planning of the 1916 Rising. During the Rising, he commanded the 2nd Battalion at Jacob's Factory on Bishop Street.

Along with Con Colbert, who also taught at St Enda's, MacDonagh was executed after the Easter Rising of 1916. Michael Collins later stayed in this house during the War of Independence.

From 1918, no. 44 (called Baerendorf) was the home of Áine Ceannt (born Frances Brennan), widow of another executed 1916 leader, Éamonn Ceannt. They were married in 1905 and she was involved in Cumann na mBan for many years prior to and following the Rising. As an anti-Treaty activist, she was jailed in Mountjoy for a year during the Civil War. She was a founder of the Irish White Cross and the organisation provided sustenance, education and benefit to the dependants of those Volunteers killed or maimed during the struggle for independence. She died in 1954.

Another staunch republican, Alec McCabe, lived in no. 33. He later founded the Educational Building Society. In no. 28 lived Thomas McCarthy, one of the founders of the Gaelic Athletic Association which met in Hayes Hotel, Thurles, in 1884. Denis McCullough, founder of the famous piano company McCullough Piggott's, lived in no. 12.

From Bloomsday to Aosdána

By a most extraordinary coincidence, another great poet, Anthony Cronin (1923–2016), lived and died in the same house, no. 30 Oakley Road (previously no. 29), from which Thomas MacDonagh left to play his fateful part in the 1916 Rising. Cronin was married to the poet and novelist Anne Haverty. Born in Enniscorthy, County Wexford, he spent much of his life in Dublin. He was a barrister, poet, novelist, biographer, critic, commentator and arts activist. With Flann O'Brien, Patrick Kavanagh and Con Leventhal, Cronin celebrated the first Bloomsday in 1954. He was advisor on arts and culture to the governments led by Charles Haughey and Garret FitzGerald during the 1980s. During this period, he was also the originator of important artistic initiatives and became a founding member of Aosdána. This organisation was established to honour those artists whose work has made an outstanding contribution to the arts in Ireland, and to encourage and assist members in devoting their energies fully to their art. He was also instrumental in the establishment of the Irish Museum for Modern Art (IMMA) and the Heritage Council.

He was honoured with Aosdána's highest accolade, becoming its first Saoi (a distinction conferred for exceptional artistic achievement) in 2003. Cronin was a member of its governing body, the Toscaireacht, until his death. He was also a member of the governing bodies of the Irish Museum of Modern Art and the National Gallery of Ireland, of which he was for a time acting chairman.

The Life of Riley and as Dead as Doornails

Cronin began his literary career as a contributor to *Envoy, A Review of Literature and Art*. He was editor of the famous and controversial literary journal *The Bell* in the 1950s and literary editor of *Time and Tide* (London). He wrote a weekly column, 'Viewpoint', in *The Irish Times* from 1974 to 1980. Later he contributed a column on poetry to the *Sunday Independent*. He also wrote several collections of poetry. His first collection of poems, called simply *Poems*, was published in 1958. Several collections followed and his *Collected Poems* was published in 2004. His poetry has been described as remarkable 'for its modernist rigour and wit, shot through with a perceptive understanding of emotional frailty'. *The End of the Modern World* (2016), written over several decades, was his final publication.

His early comic semi-autobiographical novel, *The Life of Riley*, is set against the background of the literary world of Dublin in the mid-twentieth century. This was his first novel and is regarded as a brilliantly sophisticated satire on bohemian life in Ireland at the time. His later memoir, *Dead as Doornails*, revisited the same period in a more serious vein. It is regarded as a movingly witty classic. He died in late 2016 on the eve of his ninety-third birthday and is survived by his wife, the writer Anne Haverty.

He is commemorated in Ranelagh with 'Anthony Cronin Lane', which leads onto the main Ranelagh thoroughfare.

From the Moon to a Kiss

Anne Haverty (b. 1959) is a novelist, scriptwriter, reviewer and poet. Born in Tipperary, she won the Rooney Prize for literature with her first novel *One Day as a Tiger*. She is also the author of a biography, *Constance Markievicz: Irish Revolutionary*, and a collection of poetry, *The Beauty of the Moon*. *The Far Side of a Kiss*, her second novel set in London in the 1820s, was longlisted for the Booker Prize. It was described by *The Observer* as 'costume drama in a state of salacious undress' and 'a novel absolutely littered with grabbings and peckings'. Her most recent novel is *The Free and Easy*, which takes a satiric look at the Ireland of the Celtic Tiger years and was published in 2006. She has also worked on film and radio scripts and co-directed a documentary, *The Whole World in His Hands*. Besides being a contributor to *The Irish Times*, the *TLS*, the *Daily Telegraph* and the *Sunday Independent*, she has been a visiting professor at the Adam Mickiewicz University in Poland and at TCD and has read her work widely in Ireland and abroad.

The Troubles, the Campaigner, the 'Conmen and Conwomen'

Mary Holland (1935–2004) was a journalist who covered the Troubles in Northern Ireland for three decades while working for *The Irish Times* and other newspapers. She lived on Oakley Road until her death in 2004. Born in Dover but raised in Ireland, she married a British diplomat, Ronald Higgins. They lived in Indonesia, but the marriage was eventually annulled.

She originally worked in fashion for *Vogue* magazine and then *The Observer*. She later came to prominence as one of the first British journalists to report on the rise of the Northern Ireland Civil Rights Association (NICRA) and became an increasingly prominent commentator on the affairs of the region.

In 1977 Conor Cruise O'Brien was appointed editor-in-chief of *The Observer* newspaper. O'Brien was a writer and politician who served as an Irish government minister and who was often criticised for his uncompromising opposition towards physical force in Irish republicanism. Shortly after starting as editor, O'Brien sent a memo to Holland:

> It is a very serious weakness of your coverage of Irish affairs that you are a very poor judge of Irish Catholics. That gifted and talkative community includes some of the most expert conmen and conwomen [*sic*] in the world and I believe you have been conned.

Holland subsequently left *The Observer* and joined *The Irish Times* as their Northern Ireland correspondent.

Her awards over the years have included the Prix Italia award for her television documentary on the Creggan in Derry (Creggan, 1980), and, in 1989, the Ewart-Biggs memorial prize for the promotion of peace and understanding in Ireland. She wrote and campaigned for abortion rights in Ireland and admitted, in an article on the topic of abortion, that she had had one. She died twelve days before her sixty-ninth birthday and is survived by her children with fellow journalist Eamonn McCann, Kitty and Luke, both of whom are journalists like their parents.

The Thom's Directory Institution

A famous publication, *Thom's Directory*, had links with Oakley Road, this because when the editor of that indispensable guide to Dublin businesses, roads, residents and much more, Samuel Carse, lived there.

Thom's Irish Almanac and Official Directory – to give it the original title – was first published in 1844 by Alexander Thom who had established a thriving printing business in Dublin. His father, Walter Thom, had edited and published the *Dublin Journal* from 1813 until he died in 1824. Alexander Thom expanded his directory over the next decade and included the *Dublin Street Directory* for the first time in 1852. Under his personal supervision, the directory grew in prestige and size and became, as it is today, an institution, part of Irish public and private life. In time *Thom's Directory* of Dublin was published as a separate directory, although the material also continued to be an integral part of *Thom's Directory of Ireland*. In 1960, *Thom's Dublin Street Directory* and *Thom's Commercial Directory* were first published as separate directories. Over the past forty years *Thom's Dublin Street Directory* has grown with the city, listing some 13,066 streets in the 2012 edition.

Reading in the Dark in Ranelagh

From Dublin to Derry and back again we travel with the Irish poet, novelist, critic and lecturer Seamus Deane, of Oakley Road. He is professor of English, teaches at the Notre Dame Centre in Dublin and is a member of the Royal Irish Academy. Until 1993, he was professor of modern English and American literature at UCD. He is also a founding director of the Field Day Theatre Company, the general editor of the Penguin editions of Joyce, and the author of several books, including *A Short History of Irish Literature*; *Celtic Revivals*; *Essays in Modern Irish Literature*; *The French Revolution and Enlightenment in England*; and *Strange Country: Modernity and the Nation*. Deane also edited the monumental *Field Day Anthology of Irish Writing* in three volumes, and has written four books of poetry and a novel, *Reading in the Dark* (1996), which has been translated into more than twenty languages. The latter also won the 1996 *Guardian* Fiction Prize and the 1996 South Bank Show Annual Award for Literature, is a *New York Times* notable book, won the *Irish Times* International Fiction Prize and the Irish Literature Prize in 1997, besides being shortlisted for the Booker Prize in 1996. Deane has co-edited, with Krzysztof Ziarek, a collection of essays, *Future*

Crossings: Literature between Philosophy and Cultural Studies (2001).
His book, *Foreign Affections: Essays on Edmund Burke* (2004), is volume
15 in the Critical Conditions series. Along with Breandán Mac Suibhne,
he is editor of the annual Irish Studies journal, *Field Day Review*.

Reading in the Dark is about a boy's coming of age during the Troubles
in his home city of Derry in Northern Ireland. While the narrator is
surrounded with violence, chaos, and sectarian division, Derry serves as
the place where he grows up, both physically and mentally. Despite the
surrounding events, the narrator's tone never slips into complete despair,
but maintains a sense of hope and humour throughout.

CHARLESTON AND DUNVILLE

Doing it the Charleston Way

Oakley Road brings us to Charleston Road, which dates from the mid-
nineteenth century. It was built on part of the old Wellington Orchards.
For a time, some of the fine houses (e.g. two-bay three-storey 'protected
structures' with a full flight of granite steps and displaying attractive
details) along this road were part of what was called Belgrave Park or
Charleston Terrace. For many years, a prominent building along this
road was the Wesleyan Methodist Church. The site for the church was
bought in 1854. In the late twentieth century it was sold and converted
into offices, while retaining its exterior features.

In the 1860s the poet Katherine Tynan (1861–1931) spent her early
school years at a school in no. 3 Charleston Road. She subsequently
played an important role in the Irish Literary Revival at the end of
the nineteenth century. Extraordinarily prolific, she wrote over 100
novels and also many collections of poetry. James Joyce, who for a time
lived with his family up the road from Charleston Road on Castlewood
Avenue, mentions her in *Ulysses*. William Magee (1868–1961), who
was a librarian of the National Library, resided at no. 36.

From the Battle of the Somme to Star of the Sea

Further along the road at no. 48 was the home of Mary Kettle, the
wife of poet Tom Kettle, who was killed at the Battle of the Somme in
1916. Tom Kettle was also a highly regarded and influential barrister,
economist, journalist and Home Rule MP. Mary Kettle was sister to
Hannah Sheehy Skeffington, a suffragette, trade unionist and Irish

nationalist. Another sister, Kathleen, married Frank Cruise O'Brien and was the mother of Conor Cruise O'Brien.

One of Ireland's most prominent nineteenth-century architects, J.J. McCarthy, lived in Charleston House for a number of years in the 1860s. His fame rests on the very impressive and important churches he designed in Ireland at a time when the Catholic Church was consolidating its influence. Some of his works included the Star of the Sea Church in Sandymount, St Catherine's Church in Meath Street in the Liberties, and St Saviour's Church on Dominick Street.

An Accidental Memoir – Dreams and Doormats

Just off Charleston Road is Charleston Avenue, a cul-de-sac road of very contrasting styles of architecture, mostly dating from the 1890s. One side has late-Victorian two-storey houses while across the road, from nos 20 to 31, there is a very picturesque and distinctive terrace of ten to twelve houses in mock-Tudor, half-timbered style with stained-glass window panes. It has been suggested that the houses were possibly designed by the English-born architect Thomas E. Hudman, who was a relation, through marriage, of James Pile. It was he who designed some similar houses on Sandford Road. The terrace is another of those hidden gems of Ranelagh.

Number 3 was the home for many years of the journalist and writer Nuala O'Faolain (1940– 2008), who wrote the best-selling book *Are You Somebody? The Accidental Memoir of a Dublin Woman*. She was the eldest of nine children and her father was the well-known *Evening Press* social columnist ('Dubliner's Diary') Terry O'Sullivan.

In her writings, she often discussed her frustration at the sexism and rigidity of roles in Catholic Ireland that expected her to marry and have children, of which she did neither. Her formative years coincided with the emergence of the Irish women's movement and it was said that her ability to expose misogyny in all its forms was formidable, forensic and unremitting. It has also been suggested that her feminism, forged and fought with erudition, courage and truthfulness, stemmed from a fundamental belief in social justice.

In *Are You Somebody?* she wrote candidly about her fifteen-year relationship with the journalist Nell McCafferty. She also wrote *Almost There*, a novel, and *My Dream of You*, all of which featured on the *New York Times* bestseller list. She was interviewed by RTÉ's Marian Finucane in 2008 in relation to her terminal illness. She said, 'I don't want more time. As soon as I heard I was going to die, the goodness went from life'. Some of her other quotes are very memorable, including: 'If there were nothing else, reading would – obviously – be worth living for'; 'Nature doesn't break your heart: other people do.

Yet, we cannot live apart from each other in bowers feeding on nectar. We're in this together, this getting through our lives, as the fact that we are word-users shows'; 'What makes a woman into a doormat? What makes her see some quite ordinary person as a looming Goliath? And are not these relationships such an outrage to reality that they cannot last a lifetime?'

Brainstorming at the Kitchen Table

Yet another writer, Kate Cruise O'Brien (1948–98), lived in no. 26 Charleston Avenue and Ranelagh was an inspiration for her novel, *Homesick Garden*. She was the youngest daughter of politician and diplomat Conor Cruise O'Brien. Her first book, *A Gift Horse*, was described by Sean Ó'Faoláin as having 'the seed of genius'. She was also literary editor with Poolbeg Press and her kitchen table was renowned among authors for its brain-storming sessions. This is where Cathy Kelly, Marian Keyes, Sheila O'Flanagan and many more writers would meet and consequently the house, like Nuala O'Faolain's nearby, is the setting for a host of literary memories.

In the 1860s, the artist Jeremiah Hodges Mulcahy lived at no. 17. He exhibited his landscape paintings in the Royal Hibernian Academy from 1843 to 1878.

The Revolution of Sisterhood

A long-time campaigner who has strong links with Ranelagh and has lived there for many years is Nell McCafferty. She is a journalist, playwright, civil rights campaigner and feminist. In 1984, she contributed a piece, 'Coping with the Womb and the Border', to an anthology, *Sisterhood is Global: International Women's Movement*. Her revolution was of a different kind, yet it ran parallel to the independence struggle. She was one of the founding members of the Irish Women's Liberation Movement. Irish author Colm Toibín noted that her achievement as a journalist is inseparable from feminism. Her perspective has proved that there is always another way of looking at things.

In 1990 she won a Jacob's Award for her RTÉ reports on the 1990 World Cup. In 2004 she published her autobiography, *Nell*. In it she explores her upbringing in Derry, her relationship with her parents, her fears over being gay, the joy of finding domestic bliss with writer Nuala O'Faolaoin, and the pain of losing it.

In 2009, after the publication of the Murphy Report on child abuse, Nell McCafferty confronted Archbishop Diarmuid Martin of Dublin, asking him why the Catholic Church had not 'as a gesture of redemption' relinquished titles such as 'Your Eminence' and 'Your Grace'.

The Irish Times wrote that 'Nell's distinctive voice, both written and spoken, has a powerful and provocative place in Irish society'. In 2016, she received an honorary doctorate of literature from University College Cork for 'her unparalleled contribution to Irish public life over many decades and her powerful voice in movements that have had a transformative impact on Irish society, including the feminist movement, campaigns for civil rights, for the marginalised and victims of injustice'.

The Sydney and Suffragists Connection

Not too far from Charleston Road is Chester Road. Number 2 was home to one of the famous Gifford sisters, Sydney Gifford Czira, a journalist and writer. Her sisters, Muriel and Grace, had married Thomas MacDonagh and Joseph Mary Plunkett, executed leaders of the 1916 Rising. Sydney was involved in Sinn Féin and the Irish suffragette movement. She wrote a very interesting book on personalities involved in the struggle for independence, *As Years Fly By*. She also wrote for the first women's newspaper produced in Ireland, *Bean na hÉireann*, highlighting the awful working conditions of many women in this country.

Jewellery and Paintings – A Rumble in Ranelagh

There was somewhat of a rumble in Ranelagh in August 1994 when a former resident of the nearby Hollyfield Buildings in Rathmines, Martin Cahill, was shot dead at the junction where Oxford Road meets Charleston Road. Cahill (1949–94) was a major Irish criminal who was later rehoused in Swan Grove (off Mountpleasant Avenue) after the demolition of Hollyfield. He generated a certain notoriety in the media, which dubbed him 'the General'. The name was also used by the media to discuss Cahill's activities while avoiding legal problems with libel. During his lifetime, Cahill took particular care to hide his face from the media – he would spread the fingers of one hand over his face. He and his gang infamously stole gold and diamonds with a value of over €2.55 million from O'Connor's jewellers in Harold's Cross in 1983. He was also involved in stealing some of the world's most valuable paintings from Russborough House in 1986.

On 18 August 1994, Cahill left the house at which he had been staying in at Swan Grove and began driving to a local video store to return a borrowed copy of *Delta Force 3: The Killing Game*. Upon reaching a road junction (where Oxford Road meets Charleston Road) he was repeatedly shot. In 1998, John Boorman directed a biographical film titled *The General*, starring Brendan Gleeson as Cahill. The film won the best director award at the Cannes Film Festival. The movie was based on the book by Irish crime journalist Paul Williams, who was also the crime editor of the Irish tabloid the *Sunday World*. The film *Ordinary Decent Criminal*, starring Kevin Spacey, was also loosely inspired by 'the General'.

DUNVILLE VILLAGE

That 'Star Quality'

Charleston Road connects to Dunville Village via Oakley Road. The old road of Dunville Avenue still retains a different-era, village-like atmosphere, more so than the main road through Ranelagh village. Many of the houses here were built by architect E.H. Carson at the end of the nineteenth century. An institution in the village is Morton's Supermarket at the corner of Dunville Avenue and Moyne Road. It has been extending and expanding more and more for years. It was originally just one of many corner grocery shops in Ranelagh, but it has developed to become the renowned emporium it is today. It is in the very heart of the village and thriving after more than eighty years in business (since 1934). It lends much to the village atmosphere of Ranelagh. Morton's core principle is having 'an old-fashioned, family-values-based approach of selling top quality produce sourced fresh from the markets and the best producers' and this has served its loyal customers very well over the years. Consequently, it is more than a supermarket and café; it is part of the neighbourhood, central to the village, a household name and way of life for many of the local residents and those beyond Ranelagh's boundaries.

Other well-known nearby shops include the Hardware Store and The Best of Italy. The clock over the inviting Peperina bistro adds to the stylish feel of the village. On the opposite side is a terrace, probably dating from the 1940s and displaying aspects of the architecture of mid-twentieth-century Dublin, that stretches from Rosalin's book and gift shop to the Dunville Pharmacy. Rosalin's also offers a schoolbook-covering service – now that is what's called service with a smile!

The Wow Factor – Helen's Fifty Shades of Grey

Helen Turkington, one of the country's leading and most renowned interior designers, is also located on Dunville Avenue. She knows how a home should look and feel and believes in the importance of the 'wow factor', whether for living rooms, bathrooms or anywhere. Her design consultancy business specialises in top-to-bottom refurbishment projects and she applies her talent for distinctive designs towards that luxurious look. It is her signature interiors that grace many of the luxury houses in Dublin and elsewhere. She was the lady who also introduced us to the fifty-shades-of-grey-interiors colour palette. Despite that, all colours are employed to create effect – maybe marine blue in a bathroom, olive green in a kitchen, or mauve to create warmth… The list goes on. She even has a colour named after one of her children – Florrie's Pink! Flattering lighting, flooring and ceiling, centrepieces, the location of essentials, wood and panelling techniques and many more approaches are used to create the right ambience in her projects.

Hollywood and Sheer Blarney

Maybe Rosalin's shop is an acknowledgement of a former famous resident of Dunville Avenue? This is the Hollywood star-spotter and casting director Ros Hubbard (*née* Cox), who finds that 'star quality' in actors and actresses. She once said that she lived on 'sheer blarney' until she met her husband John. Some of her films included *The Mummy*, *Enemy at the Gate*, *The Bourne Ultimatum*, *The Hobbit* and *The Lord of the Rings*, not forgetting *Father Ted* and *Angela's Ashes*. She was also involved with *The Commitments* and was given the task of finding a cast of unknowns by Alan Parker. She is credited with discovering actors such as Colin Farrell, Saoirse Ronan, Kate Winslett and Orlando Bloom. She was also known as 'queen of the commercials' and was involved in such ads as the famous one for Levi's 501s. She is still a regular at the piano at The Groucho Club in Soho.

The Charwoman's Daughter and the Crock of Gold

The writer, poet and novelist James Stephens (1880–1950) is listed in the 1913 Dublin City Electoral Roll as living in no. 20 Killeen Road, near Dunville Village. The road was then part of the 'Rathmines East' electoral area. He was a close friend of the 1916 leader Thomas MacDonagh, who worked in St Enda's School, nearby. One of his novels, *The Crock of Gold*, achieved enduring popularity. The story is a mixture of homespun philosophy, the battle of the sexes and Irish folklore. He wrote on the Easter Rising in *Insurrection in Dublin* and described the effects of the executions as 'like watching blood oozing from under a door'. One of his most well-known books, particularly among secondary-school students, is *The Charwoman's Daughter*, which vividly recounts life in Dublin's tenements around the time of the infamous Dublin Lockout of 1913.

5

LOOKING TO THE STARS – RANELAGH ROAD AND DARTMOUTH

THE OBSERVATORY

Telescopes, Periscopes and Printing Banknotes

One of the northern boundaries of Ranelagh is along the Grand Canal at Charlemont Bridge, which brings one on to Ranelagh Road. The road itself was originally called the Dublin Way, an important exit from the old medieval city to the outskirts of Dublin and on to Wicklow. Later still, an 1837 map of the area shows it as Charlemont Street Upper.

This map also shows an 'observatory' not too far from the bridge. In the early nineteenth century, the maker of scientific and astronomical instruments, Thomas Grubb (1800–78), lived at no. 1 Ranelagh Road and had his workshop nearby. Grubb was a billiard-table maker, a clockmaker, and then an optician who diversified into making intricate scientific instruments, including telescopes and lenses. In the 1830s he set up an engineering works near Charlemont Bridge, called Optical and Mechanical Works, and built himself a small observatory on the site, hence the inclusion on the map. Grubb also constructed precision instruments for Trinity College Dublin. In the early 1840s, Grubb became 'engineer of the Bank of Ireland' on College Green. He was responsible for designing and constructing machinery for engraving, printing and numbering banknotes.

When Grubb received an order to build a 48-inch reflector for Melbourne Observatory, he and his son, Howard, set up a new works nearby at Observatory Lane. The firm prospered and he built and exported some of the world's greatest telescopes, many of which are

still operational. Amongst his many achievements is the world-famous telescope in Birr Castle, Co. Offaly, which he helped to build. His telescopes are still used in Dunsink, Armagh, Greenwich observatories and elsewhere. During the First World War, Grubb Works provided most of the periscopes for the Royal Navy's submarines.

One of Dublin's Best-Known Undertakers

Not too far from Grubb's home is a laneway called Price's Lane, where an old business, McGovern's Metal Recycling, is located. It has been dealing in scrap metal for over a century. Interestingly, two of Ranelagh's other oldest businesses are across the main road. Just off Dartmouth Square, at the back of Leeson Park, is Dartmouth Lane, where Walton's Motors is located. Nearby is the Veterinary Hospital on Dartmouth Road. All three businesses have been operating for over 100 years.

Walton's is one of Dublin's best-known back-lane garages, sited near the Luas stop at Charlemont. The garage has been operational since 1924 and before that there was a forge located there, then a hackney business and an undertakers', so there is a fascinating touch of the time warp to the business. It also had the only 24-hour petrol station in the south of the city.

War of Independence and the Ryan and Colbert Families

Returning to the main thoroughfare, no. 19 Ranelagh Road was once home to a staunchly republican family, the Ryans. Min and Mary-Kate Ryan were two prominent young nationalists. Min was an activist in 1916 and during the War of Independence. The house served as a meeting place for the GHQ staff of the Irish Volunteers, and was where Seán T. O'Kelly spent the night before the Rising. On Holy Thursday 1916, Min was tasked with bringing a message to Wexford that was to signal the start of the Rising, but on Good Friday Eoin MacNeill sent her back again with a message to cancel. When the Rising eventually did start on Easter Monday, the two sisters joined the rebels in the GPO.

Min was romantically involved with Seán MacDermott (one of the leaders who was captured and executed by the British). In one of his final letters from Kilmainham Jail, he told his family that 'if I think of any other things to say I will tell them to Miss Ryan, she who in all probability, had I lived, would have been my wife.' Min and her sister were his last visitors before his execution by firing squad in the early hours of 12 May 1916. Min later married General Richard (Dick) Mulcahy, who served as chief-of-staff of the IRA during the War of Independence. One of their sons was the eminent cardiologist Dr Risteard Mulcahy. A sister, Phyllis, married Seán T. Kelly, another activist and later President of Ireland.

Number 28 Ranelagh Road was the home where Con Colbert, one of those executed in 1916, also stayed. He had moved at the age of 16 from his home in Limerick to live with his sister in Ranelagh. Today this is called Colbert House. During the 1916 Rising, Colbert fought at Watkin's Lane Brewery, Marrowbone Lane and Jameson Distillery, all in the Liberties. His brother Jim Colbert was also involved in the republican cause, while living with his wife, Roisín, in Alban House on Albany Road, also in Ranelagh. They made the house available to the Irish Volunteers during the War of Independence and it was a well-used 'safe house' for Michael Collins, Seán Russell, Frank Aiken Seán MacBride.

The film producer and historian of Irish film, Liam O'Leary, lived for many years in no. 74.

DARTMOUTH SQUARE

An Architectural Set Piece

Between Ranelagh Road and Upper Leeson Street is Dartmouth Square, containing a significant historical park from the late Victorian/early Edwardian period, situated in the centre of a quiet tree-lined residential enclave. The park boundary is still defined by its original wrought-iron railings and gates. The dominant built feature of the park is its pergola and pathway. The square itself is the last of a series of formal Victorian residential squares which were laid out in Dublin in the nineteenth century.

Rectangular in shape, and originally part of the Darley estate, Dartmouth Square comprises a central park of approximately 2 acres, surrounded by two-storey-over-basement red-brick Victorian houses. The landscaped central area, with its mature shrubbery and trees, provides a contrast to the surrounding uniform terraces of houses. This sylvan character also gives the area a secluded atmosphere and a welcome feeling of separation from the not-too-far away urban hustle and bustle. It has been suggested that, consequently, the square links city dwellers to the natural world and the changing rhythm of seasons. Moreover, in an increasingly environmentally conscious world, the benefits of parks with mature trees in urban areas, such as Dartmouth and the nearby Mount Pleasant Square, for a healthy and sustainable city environment, are becoming more recognised and appreciated. They become part of the vital and indispensable ecological chain as well as being an integral part of the architectural set piece.

Exodus – Movement of the People

The development of Dartmouth Square coincided with the movement of the middle classes from the city to the suburbs. Suburban growth generally commenced in Dublin from the beginning of the nineteenth century. Part of the site was offered by the developer and owner of the land, Mr Darley, to the Rathmines Urban District Council as a 'scavenging station' or dump, as it had been so used for many years. However, wiser counsels prevailed and it was earmarked for residential development. The Darley family built the houses as part of a speculative development and plans were drawn up as early as the 1870s. The houses are noteworthy for many reasons, in particular for the quality and high standard of design and materials used. Whereas Mount Pleasant Square on the opposite side of Ranelagh Road was laid out in the early nineteenth century, Dartmouth Square was not laid out until the late nineteenth century. The squares consequently reflect the different architectural fashions and styles. Mount Pleasant is more Georgian in composition. Dartmouth is red-bricked, late Victorian and displays features of the era, such as recessed porches. A striking feature throughout Dartmouth Square is the flight of granite steps leading up to front doors.

All for Hecuba – From Monto to the Shaking Hand of Dublin

Alfie Byrne, nine times Lord Mayor of Dublin (1930–39 and 1954–55), and known as 'the shaking hand of Dublin' because of his political skills and friendliness, lived in no. 23 in the 1920s. He was a popular politician and liked to cycle around the city on his sturdy bike. He was well dressed and sported a well-maintained waxed moustache. The founder of the Legion of Mary, Frank Duff, who was credited (wrongly) with bringing about the demise of the notorious red-light district of Dublin, Monto, lived in no. 51, also in the 1920s. Joseph Michael O'Byrne SC lived in no. 55. He was a 1916 veteran (Boland's Mills) and later registrar of deeds. Hilton Edwards and Michael Mac Liammóir of the Gate Theatre lived in no. 61 in the 1930s before moving to Harcourt Terrace. In their book, *All for Hecuba,* they recalled Dartmouth Square and stated, 'our life in the quiet house proved quite pleasant'.

O'Hara, O'Mara, O'Shaughnessy and an Oscar

Next door in no. 62 lived Thomas Lopdell O'Shaughnessy, recorder for Dublin. Other noteworthy figures who lived on the square included Power O'Mara of the Globe Theatre Company and son of opera singer Joseph O'Mara. Barry Fitzgerald (born William Joseph Shields), who was an actor with the Abbey Theatre and who later appeared in *The Quiet Man* with John Wayne and fellow Ranelagh-resident Maureen O'Hara, also lived on the square. He was an Oscar-winning actor. Donagh MacDonagh (1912–68), son of Irish patriot Thomas MacDonagh, was a poet, playwright and short-story writer, and lived here for a time. Another prominent resident was Professor Kevin B. Nowlan of UCD (known to all as 'KB'). He was a conservation supremo and veteran of many battles to save Dublin's historic fabric (including Wood Quay) and historical places.

The Cardinal, the Wife and the Television

Paul Durcan (b. 1944), the well-known poet, was born in no. 57 and raised partly in Ranelagh and County Mayo. Durcan published his first collection of poetry in 1975 and has been writing to critical acclaim ever since. He has been awarded both the Patrick Kavanagh Award and the 1990 Whitbread Prize (for his collection *Daddy, Daddy*). He was influenced by the era in which he grew up – sometimes regarded as culturally and socially bleak, conservative, challenging, with hypocrisy and corruption in the higher social classes of Irish society. It has been suggested that those times may have seemed antagonistic and malignant to the creative mind. His fraught relationship with his father and his experience of the Irish psychiatric system also had a profound influence. In addition to being a public poet, commenting on social institutions and mores, Durcan has written a body of poetry dealing with more personal issues, such as 'The Laughter of Mothers'; he is a master of the lyrical as well as the satirical voice and has a sharp, dry wit, evident in some of his poetry. Many of his poems are set in Dublin and engage with current politics and society, sometimes to comic effect. 'Our world is strange because it has no future ...' comes from the poem, 'The Girl with the Keys to Pearse's Cottage'. It captures the mood of endemic emigration that was a pervading feature of most of twentieth-century Ireland. Another poem, 'The Wife Who Smashed Television Sets', reflects on the unusual relationship between Church and state to the detriment of the citizen and women in particular. Other poems deal with this theme, including 'Cardinal Dies of Heart Attack in Dublin Brothel'. A period of intense creativity is highlighted in collections of poetry such as 'O Westport in the Light of Asia Minor', 'Teresa's Bar' and 'Sam's Cross'. Interestingly, as with Luke Kelly, he counts Patrick Kavanagh (and also T.S. Eliot) among his literary muses. He shares many of Kavanagh's contradictory views on Ireland.

He was related to the MacBride political family, through his mother, Sheila Durcan MacBride, a niece of Major John MacBride.

Luke Kelly and the Importance of Simplicity

Luke Kelly (1940–84), of *The Dubliners* folk and ballad group, lived at no. 7 until his early death. He was one of the founding members of that world-famous group. He was noted for his distinctive singing style and is often regarded as one of Ireland's greatest folk singers. According to fellow *Dubliners* member, the late Ronnie Drew, Luke 'learnt to sing with perfect diction'. It was said that his political beliefs and strong left-leaning tendencies gave a certain edge and conviction to his singing and lent weight to the groups' repertoire. In the early 1960s the ballad boom took off in Ireland and by this time Luke, having met and played with Ronnie Drew and others in O'Donoghue's Pub on Baggot Street, suggested they call the new group *The Dubliners*, after the book of the same name by James Joyce, which he was reading at the time. In 1965 he married Deirdre O'Connell, founder of the Focus Theatre. There are some songs in particular often associated with Luke Kelly – 'The Town I Loved So Well', 'Raglan Road', 'Hand Me Down My Bible' and 'Scorn Not His Simplicity', a song about composer Phil Coulter's son who had Down's Syndrome. He had such respect for this song that he only recorded it once for television and avoided singing it at *The Dubliners'* often wild and raucous concerts. 'Raglan Road', the name of a road just a short walk from Dartmouth Square, was originally a poem written by Patrick Kavanagh. He had

heard Luke Kelly singing in The Bailey pub, off Grafton Street, and asked him to sing the poem to the music of 'The Dawning of the Day'. Luke obliged. He died in 1984 after succumbing to the effects of a brain tumour. His legacy and contribution to Irish music and culture have been described as 'iconic'.

On the Tiles – The Battle for Dartmouth Square

The square became the subject of controversy in 2005, when it emerged that a few years previously a businessman had bought the freehold on the square for £10,000 from P.J. Darley, a descendant of the square's builders. In 2006 the gates of the park were locked against the residents and the businessman tried to use the area as a car park and for selling tiles. After three years of dispute with residents and Dublin City Council, an agreement was negotiated to reopen it to be used as an amenity again. The local community gathered regularly to clean up the square which was in a state of ruin after years without any maintenance. After a couple of months and a big effort, it was returned it to its former glory. Local community members also gave money to get in heavy machinery to cut back all the overgrowth, paint benches and get rid of the graffiti. On 11 June 2009, it was reopened with great celebrations, and on 13 June the first outdoor yoga class took place, followed by a summer of events, such as silent cinema with live music, poetry evenings, children's parties, charity fundraisers and many more cultural events. In September 2009 singer Damien Rice took part in a tree-planting initiative with Trinity College students, planting thirty-two apple and pear trees.

In December 2012, the square was sold at auction on instruction of the liquidator of Marble Tile and Granite. Dublin City Council and a group of local residents paid for the square at this auction and donated it back to DCC. Finally, after years of dispute over its ownership, it became public property again. The square is now wholly owned by Dublin City Council.

The Asylum and the Lost Weekend

Northbrook Road dates from the 1860s and 1870s and was originally named Read's Road after the developer. The most striking building on this quiet road was originally the Old Men's Asylum, now called the Northbrook Clinic. This striking building dates from 1864 and is a Gothic revival institution. It has a strong symmetrical design and is entered through a porch under a tower. It was designed by William G. Murray and was built 'to provide a comfortable home for 25 respectable, reduced, aged Protestant men of good character'. The governor of the asylum was a Captain Hackett who lived nearby at 1 Cambridge Terrace on the corner site with Dartmouth Square.

Northbrook Road and the Old Men's Asylum/Northbrook Clinic, 1864.
(Courtesy of the *Dublin Builder*/NLI)

Another old establishment still located nearby at no. 5 Northbrook Road is the Carr's Child and Family Services. This home was originally established by a Miss Lizzie Hawthorne Carr, a philanthropic lady who was appalled that in the early 1880s there were 5,000 'neglected, abandoned or orphaned' children living in industrial schools in Ireland. She wanted to do something for destitute children and her first home was established in 1887. In 1920, she bought the Victorian property at Northbrook Road, which housed twenty-four children and was known as Carr's Children's Home. It operated as such until 2007. The main focus of the organisation today is on working with families.

Nearby was the former Northbrook Hotel, a famous but little-known late-night boîte – a haunt for late-night revellers. It was said that a few lost hours in this family run establishment could quickly turn into a lost weekend.

The Joly Inventor

Professor John Joly (1857–1933) of Trinity College Dublin lived in no. 12 Northbrook Road, and was regarded as one of Ireland's foremost scientists. Among his many achievements is the Joly colour process, which was the first successful process for producing colour images from a single photographic plate. Joly also invented a photometer for measuring light intensity, a meldometer for measuring the melting points of minerals, a differential steam calorimeter for measuring specific heats and a constant-volume gas thermometer. All these bear his name.

The Irish Congress of Trade Unions and the Irish Hotels Federation both had offices on Northbrook Road over the years.

LEESON PARK

Con, Beckett and the Blasphemy of Joyce

Leeson Park marks one of the boundaries of Ranelagh with the wider world and this spacious tree-lined street, replete with large, somewhat stately Victorian red-bricks, mostly accessed by flights of steps, dates from the 1860s. The name derives from Joseph Leeson, 1st Earl of Milltown (1701–83).

A resident who lived at no. 51 Leeson Park was Abraham Jacob Leventhal (1896–1979), widely known as 'Con' Leventhal. He was a lecturer in French at Trinity College Dublin and a well-known art,

drama and literary critic, as well as broadcaster. After the First World War, he was among those who worked for the first Zionist Commission in Palestine. Upon returning to Dublin in the 1920s he founded a literary journal, *The Klaxon*. Samuel Beckett was a regular contributor and good friend, which led to Leventhal later working for him as a secretary.

He was born in Dublin in 1896, and educated at Wesley College. His childhood experiences in Catholic Dublin are recounted with humour and poignancy in *What It Means to Be a Jew*. His undergraduate studies at Trinity College were interrupted when he joined the first Zionist Commission immediately after the First World War and spent a year in Palestine, where he helped to found the *Palestine Weekly*. He was invited to join the London office of the Jewish National Fund where he became associated with the *Zionist Review*. Returning to Dublin to take up his academic studies, he recognised immediately the remarkable talent of his fellow Dubliner, James Joyce, of whose work he remarked, 'the riches are embarrassing'. Leventhal submitted a review of *Ulysses* to the *Dublin Magazine* (this was to mark the beginning of a literary association and deep personal friendship with its editor Seamus O'Sullivan that was to last until O'Sullivan died, and with him his famous magazine, in 1958), but as he corrected the galley sheets word came that the printers in Dollards would down tools rather than take part in the publication of the blasphemous writings of Joyce. He later interviewed Joyce in Paris on the day of the publication of *Ulysses*. He was married three times and died in 1979.

Last Surviving Member of the First Dáil

Seán MacEntee (1889–1984), a former Fianna Fáil government minister, lived at no. 9 Leeson Park. He was one of the founders of that party. In a career that spanned over forty years as a Fianna Fáil TD, MacEntee was one of the most important figures in post-independence Ireland. He had fought in the GPO garrison during the 1916 Easter Rising, and was sentenced to death, but this was commuted to life imprisonment. He served in the governments of Éamon de Valera and Seán Lemass in a range of ministerial positions, including finance, industry and commerce, and health. He was a member of every Fianna Fáil cabinet from 1932 to April 1965. He and Lemass introduced a protectionist policy from 1932 that was later reversed due to the pivotal influence of T.K. Whitaker, public servant and economist. It was said that MacEntee's poor grasp of economics did not help his political career and may have been a factor in Seán Lemass succeeding de Valera. MacEntee was appointed to the Ministry of Health with Lemass retaining control of the financial and economic portfolios. He was later appointed Tánaiste when Seán Lemass was appointed Taoiseach. He is credited during this period with the reorganisation of the health services, the establishment of separate departments of health and social welfare, and the fluoridation of water supplies in Ireland. MacEntee retired from Dáil Éireann in 1969 at the age of 80, which made him the oldest TD in Irish history. At the time of his death, in 1984, aged 94, he was the last surviving member of the first Dáil. His daughter was the Irish poet Máire Mhac an tSaoi. She was married to the politician Conor Cruise O'Brien.

The Irish Management Institute was located at no. 12 from 1956 to 1963. The Construction Industry Federation was at no. 9 for a number of years, before moving to its present site near Charlemont Bridge, overlooking the Grand Canal. Both organisations have been pivotal in Ireland's economic success story.

A Chorus of Approval

The Leeson Park Players, an amateur music and dramatic society, have strong links with Christ Church, Leeson Park, that imposing structure on the corner with Leeson Street and Dartmouth Road, and have been performing theatrical masterpieces since 1933. Every year they present two productions. Starting with *The Patsy* in 1933, productions over the following years included *The Flint Street Nativity*, *The White-headed Boy*, *The Parson Says 'No'*, *The Brontës of Haworth Parsonage*, *Ladies in Retirement*, *Queen Elizabeth Slept Here*, *Mrs Moonlight*, *A Doll's House*, *The Winslow Boy*, *How the Other Half Loves*, *All in Favour Said 'No!'*, *Lady Windermere's Fan*, and *A Chorus of Disapproval*. As recently as December 2016, they presented *Eloise is Under the Almond Tree*, a Spanish comedy be Enrique Jardiel Poncela.

DUBLIN'S GOLDEN AGE AND HEDONISM

Leeson and Pimping Peg

We now return to Ranelagh Road and Joseph Leeson, who had a house on that road, a house that he used for a particular purpose and a particular person. Leeson has a very interesting and unusual association with the area. He is remembered in adjoining street names such as Leeson Street and Leeson Park in Ranelagh itself. In the late eighteenth century, when Dublin was experiencing a golden age of confidence and prosperity, one of those most notorious young 'bucks' who frequented Daly's gambling club on College Green was John 'Buck' Lawless. His notoriety also revolved around his role for many years as a lover of Margaret Leeson (née Plunkett) who became the vice-queen of Georgian Dublin, an era famed for its hedonistic approach to life. She was one of the eighteenth century's most flamboyant characters. She is also sometimes regarded as Ireland's first brothel-owning 'madam' (aka 'Pimping Peg'), and she was a fascinating woman. Clever, witty and beautiful, she was a leading figure in the hedonist set of Georgian Dublin and she counted lords, lawyers and bankers among her clientele. For many years, she was the talk of the town, what with her jewellery, her dresses, her carriages, her clients, her girls and, above all, her attitude.

From 'Game Cock Joe' to Ranelagh

A very independent-minded person, from the age of 15 (after she became pregnant and was abandoned by her upper-class seducer), Margaret Plunkett effectively navigated upper-class society to ensure her survival. First, she was the 'kept woman' of a succession of wealthy men, and later the operator of a lucrative, high-end brothel frequented by the rich and famous of the day. Not for her conventional marriage involving a life of docility and subservience. She regarded marriage as an unfair contract. She met Joseph Leeson, a wealthy English merchant from whom she took her assumed name to enhance her respectability. He was known as 'Game Cock Joe', son and heir to the 1st Earl of Milltown. He had a house on Ranelagh Road. Leeson fell for her charms and put her up in his Ranelagh home. However, while Leeson was away, she would sneak into the house of her other lover, Buck Lawless. Leeson finally found out and abandoned her. Buck Lawless went on to become her longest client and partner and they lived together for five years, having five children. However, as ever, tragedy struck; their money eventually ran out, the children died one by one and Lawless absconded for America, leaving Margaret heartbroken. Nonetheless, she kept for social-standing purposes the name of her first 'keeper' and so styled herself 'Margaret Leeson'. She never married subsequently but had various relationships. She was later to write in her memoirs that with regard to Joseph Leeson, she was more 'distressed by the loss of his purse than the loss of his person'.

The Pinking Dindies and Services Rendered

With the departure of Buck Lawless, she returned to a life of prostitution and found that many wealthy men were willing to entertain her and pay her way. She soon regained her position in high society and her first brothel in Dublin was opened on Drogheda Street (now O'Connell Street). However, this brothel was closed owing to an attack by the Pinking Dindies. It was Richard Crosbie (1755–1800), the famous duellist and aeronaut (he famously ascended from a balloon in Ranelagh Gardens), who led the gang to wreck her brothel. Not to be deterred, on receiving compensation from Crosbie, she continued her business elsewhere (just off Grafton Street on the site of what is now the Westbury Hotel). Extremely astute, she later became friends with Crosbie and shook his hand publicly before his historic balloon flight.

Her brothel became a popular establishment amongst well-bred men and her clients included a lord lieutenant (Charles Manners, 4th Duke

of Rutland and lord lieutenant of Ireland, known for his convivial nature and ample banquets in Dublin Castle. Rutland Square, now Parnell Square, was named after him. He insisted on sleeping only with Margaret, swearing he would pay his fortune if only his wife was as good in bed as she was. She refused, however, to have as a client another lord lieutenant, John Fane, the Earl of Westmoreland, because of his ill treatment of his wife. The famous banker, a Huguenot called David La Touche, whose name still lives on in Dublin financial circles (and is the official name for Portobello Bridge), was the governor of the Bank of Ireland and likewise a very important visitor to her brothels. She also listed among her clients earls, generals, top barristers, merchants, aldermen, writers, clergymen, and many at the top levels of every influential area of society. One of these was a Revenue official with a wooden leg who was brought to court, successfully, to force him to pay his debts of £50 for services rendered.

Manners and Masquerades

When Signor Carnavalli (a celebrated violinist) came to the Smock Alley Theatre to perform Italian operas, he barred certain kinds of people from attending, or as Peg put it, 'every lady of my description'. She turned up at the theatre nonetheless and took her usual seat but, on Carnavalli's orders, was unceremoniously thrown out by the doormen. Furious at this ill treatment, she got a warrant against them for assault and robbery (for holding the ticket she had paid for) and returned to the theatre with four of the nastiest bailiffs she could find, who then hauled Carnavalli and the doormen off to Newgate Prison.

An outspoken and shrewd woman, Margaret Leeson is perhaps best summed up by this story: one night, Charles Manners (the lord lieutenant), one of her most important clients, appeared in the regal box at the theatre (Smock Alley) on the same night that Peg was attending the show with her girls. Some characters in the gallery began shouting

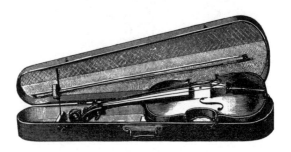

at her, 'Oy Peg! Who slept with you last night, Peg?' Peg gave them an imperious look, threw a dramatic glance at the lord lieutenant and, in a scolding tone, said, 'Manners, you dogs!'

The Sham Squire, Ruffians and Revenge

In the early 1790s, after thirty years in the business, Margaret Leeson decided to retire and cash in all the promissory notes she had accumulated. However, she became penniless in the process, as former clients refused to pay or had disappeared. Consequently, she ended up in a debtors' prison. By this time, she had also lost her once strikingly beautiful looks. However, a few of her former admirers did help her. Francis Higgins ('the Sham Squire'), the owner of the *Freeman's Journal*, did provide some assistance. Bishop Harvey of Derry, who was also the Earl of Bristol and a former client, likewise sent her some money. Despite this, she attempted suicide, and after the failed attempt, she wrote her memoirs in a bid to raise some cash (and gain some revenge!). She wrote *The Memoirs of Mrs Leeson, Written by Herself*, published between 1795 and '97. Two volumes appeared, to the embarrassment of many, while she was still alive. In these memoirs, she also complains that Dublin was home to many men who 'however they might be deemed gentlemen at their birth, or connections, yet, by their actions, deserved no other appellation than that of RUFFIANS'. The brutal realities of life in eighteenth-century Dublin are captured in the final chapter of the life of Margaret Lesson, who died following a rape and the resulting complications of venereal disease from which she did not recover. She died at the age of 70, at Fownes Street, Temple Bar, broken and alone. It has been said that a guard of honour at her funeral would have stretched from Parliament House to Dublin Castle.

6

OLD MOUNT PLEASANT, THE SQUARE AND HELL'S KITCHEN

MOUNT PLEASANT

Confusingly Pleasant

Continuing along the Ranelagh Road brings us to the Mount Pleasant area of Ranelagh, which contains some of its oldest properties. In relation to the spelling of its name, it may be somewhat confusing or charming to a visitor, depending on one's mood at any one time. Sometimes it's spelt Mount Pleasant, as in Mount Pleasant Square, yet other times it's spelt Mountpleasant, particularly in relation to the less salubrious avenues and byways. Maybe there is no rhyme nor reason for this apparent inconsistency and maybe it's to turn us all into philosophers or jabbering idiots, depending on how much time we spend mulling over the issue. Or maybe we should merely think of the words of Oscar Wilde when he was in the gutter. The esteemed Deirdre Kelly, in her history of the area, *Four Roads to Dublin*, suggests that Mount Pleasant may have derived its name either from having a pleasant view from that hilltop out to the sea, or from Thomas Pleasants, a Huguenot builder who lived near here.

Thomas Grub may well have been looking at the stars from the Ranelagh Road but housing developers in the late eighteenth and early nineteenth centuries were looking at nearer views from the slopes overlooking the Swan River and Ranelagh Road. They were admiring the views of Dublin city and beyond to Dublin Bay from the mounts or hillocks in the area. The developers were cognisant of the whispers and the needs of the burgeoning middle classes, who would have been also impressed with the possibilities for fresh air, an improvement on the unhealthy and tenement-filled city, particularly after the Act of Union of 1800 when the 'rich marched out and the poor marched in', consequently creating the overcrowded conditions in the city centre. Always alert, the developers tapped into this need and facilitated many of the influential middle classes' ambitions to live beyond the canals, in fresher and healthier pastures and in keeping with their status. The Mount Pleasant vicinity, near Ranelagh Gardens and Willbrook House, was ripe for such development.

The Salmon Leap and Donnybrook Fair

Development had already started in Ranelagh as, overlooking Ranelagh Gardens, three terraces dating from the late eighteenth century – Selskar, Manders and Old Mount Pleasant – were already in place. An unusual feature of Selskar and Manders terraces is the collection of long front gardens descending to Ranelagh Road, each with a gated entrance along the old brick wall fronting the road. The noted landscape artist William Sadlier lived in no. 3 Manders Terrace. Some of his paintings include 'A View of the Salmon Leap, Leixlip', which is in the National Gallery of Ireland, and 'Donnybrook Fair'. He died in Ranelagh in 1839.

Beside these two terraces is Old Mount Pleasant, a terrace of ten houses on the crest of the slope, just off Mount Pleasant Square. The terrace is partially hidden behind Ranelagh multi-denominational school. These ten houses in Old Mount Pleasant are a mixture of brick-fronted, two-storey and three-storey houses, some with basements. At the end of the terrace is no. 1, a Victorian-era pub, The Hill, which now incorporates its neighbour, no. 2, into the premises.

Ivory the Architect

In the middle of the terrace, no. 6 is a most interesting-looking house dating from the 1770s. It was probably the first to be built and would have been detached for a number of years. The house was the home of Thomas Ivory, the eighteenth-century architect who designed the King's Hospital, now the headquarters of the Incorporated Law Society; the Newcomen Bank, now the Dublin City Council's Rates Office; and other fine buildings. He was one of the most important architects working in Dublin in the latter decades of the eighteenth century when the city was experiencing its 'golden age'. He is commemorated with a plaque on the wall of the Rates Office, which states that he was the first drawing master of the School of Drawing in Architecture at the Dublin Society. Ivory lived at no. 6 from 1775 until his death in 1786. An image of Thomas Ivory himself survives in the King's Hospital.

Painted by John Trotter, it shows Ivory sitting at a table with maps, books and drawings, in the company of fellow experts and planners. This terrace remains an interesting and curious part of Dublin's architectural heritage.

The Curved Square and the Green Dome

Completed in 1834, Mount Pleasant Square is widely celebrated for its elegance and quiet charm. In an article on Dublin's Georgian Squares, long-time Ranelagh resident Susan Roundtree noted, 'It has justifiably been described as one of the most beautiful nineteenth century squares in Dublin'. Her views were echoed by Gordon Lynch writing in the *In Dublin* magazine in 1979, who added that 'the recently face-lifted Mount Pleasant Square, which is protected by a preservation order, is the only curved square in Dublin, if such a thing is possible'. Archiseek described it as 'one of the most charming enclaves of Georgian houses in the city'. Even the late architectural historian Maurice Craig added his praise, regarding it as one of Dublin's finest squares. Moreover, a distinctive and unusual addition to a vista of the square is the massive green dome towering behind, and yet over, the square.

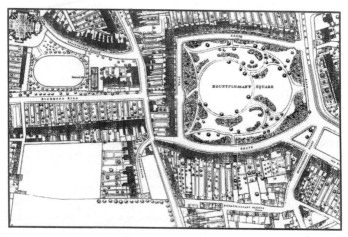

Mount Pleasant Square in the 1870s. (Courtesy of UCD Map Library)

From Glove Making to Georgian Terraces

The overall composition of the square is quite impressive. There are fifty-six handsome terraced Georgian houses in a development of two-, three- and four-storey-over-basement houses that curve around a park in a semi-circle. This was one of the first suburban developments built in the city after the Act of Union of 1800 – between the years 1803 and 1834. It was the Dolan family who developed Mount Pleasant Square. Terence Dolan was a glove maker from Chester in England who, in the early 1800s, had bought plots of land in the vicinity from Solomon Williams. His son, Terence Thomas Dolan was, like Frederick Stokes, who was a prominent speculative developer in Portobello and Rathmines, keenly involved in the establishment of the unionist-dominated Rathmines Township. This was essentially a local government enterprise covering the wider area, but, crucially, independent of the remit of the nationalist-dominated Dublin Corporation. The first houses built by Dolan, on the south side of the square, because of the raised elevation of the site had commanding views of the city centre. He leased this first tranche of houses and used the money to buy more land in the immediate vicinity, the north and west sides of the future square. By 1848, Dolan Jnr, a solicitor, owned thirty-two houses on the square. Doctors and lawyers were among some of the first inhabitants as the location was conveniently close to their offices and rooms on nearby Fitzwilliam and Merrion squares.

Letterboxes and Luminaries

Dolan Jnr lived in no. 31, the largest house on the square, with an archway through the ground floor area that leads directly to Mountpleasant Avenue, Richmond Hill and Rathmines Road. There is also a second entrance to this avenue, this time via nos 35 and 35a. His son, Henry Joseph Dolan, became president of the Mount Pleasant Lawn Tennis Club, in the middle of the square, when it was established in 1893. Today, no. 31 is gifted with eight letterboxes, one for each panel of the front door. Across from the entrance to the house, a former pedestrian gate into the park has been locked for many years. Towering trees of all types block any view over the square from no. 31 and the rest of the houses at each side. In the 1911 Census, there were 387 people living on the square, an average of seven people per house, which would have included domestic servants.

The north and south sides are crescents rather than typical borders of a square. The three-sided 'square' is, consequently, rather a semicircular development, and is unfortunately mostly hidden with an *ad hoc* mixture of tennis courts, a pavilion, towering poles and spotlights, and tall trees, all very attractive and useful in their own rights, but obstructing a vista of the wider area. Deirdre Kelly was full of admiration for the old public lighting, the brickwork and the gentle curves that combined to make this 'a lovely square'.

That We May Face the Rising Sun

One of the preeminent Irish writers of the twentieth century, John McGahern, used the curved north terrace of Mount Pleasant Square as the cover of his book, *The Pornographer*. He has captivated readers with such poignant and heart-wrenching novels as *Amongst Women*, *That They May Face the Rising Sun* and *The Dark*. Maybe it was the dark and the tree-shrouded area where the sun never seems to shine that inspired him. In *The Pornographer*, the main character, Michael, creates an ideal world of sex while working as a writer of pornographic fiction. Meanwhile he bungles every phase of his entanglement with an older woman who has the misfortune to fall in love with him. But his insensitivity to this love is in direct contrast to the tenderness with which he attempts to make his aunt's slow death in a hospital tolerable. Everywhere in this rich novel is the drama of opposites, but above all, sex and death are never far from each other as McGahern explores the layers and shades of our emotions and our relationships.

MOUNTPLEASANT BUILDINGS

Hell's Kitchen and the Hill

Mount Pleasant has always been like that – an area of contrasts – whether it be personalities or politics, unionist or nationalist, rich or poor, poverty or affluence. It still has those contrasts to this day and for some it helps give the area a somewhat 'cosmopolitan' atmosphere. Until the 1970s only a few roads separated the prosperous Mount Pleasant Square from Mountpleasant Buildings, which was a complex of hastily built tenements, a slum of squalor and poverty that nestled behind Mountpleasant Avenue, Oxford Road, Mountpleasant Place and Alma Terrace. This hidden enclave has long since been demolished. The area is unrecognisable today, with the Dublin Corporation having built houses on the site.

The tenements, variously known as 'the Buildings', 'Hell's Kitchen' and 'the Hill', were originally built between 1901 and 1931 by Dublin Corporation for the working classes transferred from the city centre – and brought there also to service the needs of the aspiring new middle classes. The 'Buildings' consisted of 246 flats – 60 one-roomed, 150 two-roomed, and 36 three-roomed. However, they were built in isolation with no social or sporting amenities and tenants lived in crowded conditions. Also, problem families from all over the city were dumped together on this little island. The place was absolutely teeming with children. Generally, the buildings were known as 'the Hill', with the worst parts at the back near Mountpleasant Avenue, which had no toilets or sinks, known as 'Hell's Kitchen'. Here, families had to go downstairs to avail of communal facilities.

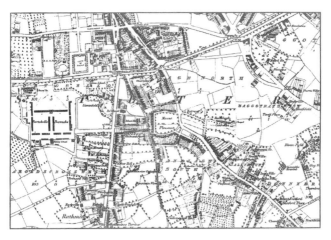

Ranelagh and environs in 1837. (Courtesy of UCD Map Library)

Stolen Hearts and Stanley Knives in Handbags

Soon, antisocial behaviour became the order of the day and 'the Buildings' acquired an unenviable reputation, particularly from the 1940s onwards. Gang violence was common, and teenagers from 'softer' surrounding suburbs fled in terror and groaned upon hearing stories about the gangs. Girlfriends of these gang members were equally notorious, and were reputed to carry Stanley and flick knives in their handbags. Moreover, they would quickly set their bulldog boyfriends on anyone, if they didn't like the look of them. There were reports of local students living in nearby 'Flatland' being frequently set up by gangs wielding bottles, frying pans, belts and metal bars. After any attack the gangs would disappear into their nearby horror haven. *The Irish Times* published an article, 'Living in Fear in Ranelagh', describing the gang violence and talking about local elderly residents being robbed. One old lady returned to a vandalised flat to find a statue of the Sacred Heart stolen. 'Ah, they've no heart at all', bemoaned one local.

Stone Age Times and 'a Woeful Place'

In the 1960s Telefís Éireann (as RTÉ was called) broadcast a documentary about the area – *Dublin Poverty: Mountpleasant Buildings*. Life was arduous and often dangerous in the slums of Mountpleasant, the documentary noted. Communal toilets were poorly maintained, overflowing rubbish bins were infested with rats, and cold, lung-choking air seeped through the damp brick walls; it was little wonder that Irish infant mortality rates were among the highest in Europe at the time. Residents described the situation as 'desperate', children as 'prone to sickness', tiny cramped conditions with 'husband, wife, teenage boy and girl all having to share – no privacy', 'toilet facilities – a basin'. They talked about having to use chair-beds. Alcoholism and family break-ups were a common feature. Asthma in children was on the increase. There were no bathrooms, no gas, no running water. For cooking facilities, many had to use the fire. Because of the cold, families spent most of their time in one room. One resident described it as 'an awful place with a communal toilet and wash-house'. Another said it was 'a woeful place to live in'. By the mid-1970s the buildings were deemed 'unfit for human habitation' and the ten blocks were to be demolished over a number of years. The former residents were scattered to the wind property values in the area rose. The poor were marched out and the rich marched in. In place of the demolished flats the Corporation built low-density social housing around the new area of what is Swan Grove, Alma Court, Rugby Villas and along Oxford Road.

Goodbye to the Hill and Goodbye to the Book!

Former resident of the Mountpleasant Buildings Lee Dunne (b. 1934) wrote his best-selling book *Goodbye to the Hill* in 1965. It was an account of his experiences of growing up in the Mountpleasant Buildings area. It was banned, however, due to its explicit sexual content.

Moreover, Dunne has been described as 'the most banned author in Ireland', with one of his novels being the last piece of literature to be banned, in 1976. Despite that, *Goodbye to the Hill* went on to sell over a million copies. In 1978 it was made into a stage play and had a twenty-six-week run, which was unheard of at the time, four weeks being the usual. Many readers of his book will relate to the story of Paddy Maguire, the universal adolescent in bondage to a self-image he detests because of the strong resemblance to a child he is anxious to outgrow. The uplifting story is all about his growing into adolescence in poverty-stricken Mountpleasant Buildings in the late 1930s and '40s. Paddy is portrayed as a lustful, thirsty and hard-working lad, a memorable character with a young life full of adventure, choice language and enough colourful incidents to create a humorous canvas.

Ranelagh's Hedy Lamarr and Hollywood

Another famous resident of 'the Buildings' was film star Constance Smith (1928– 2003), who lived there in the 1930s and '40s. She was born to Mary Biggane, a Limerick native, and Sylvester Smith, a former soldier in the English Army and veteran of the First World War. He, a Dubliner, worked at the Ardnacrusha Power Plant on the River Shannon in the late 1920s, when the river was being harnessed to generate electricity, a huge undertaking at the time which was to bring major benefits to the economy and to rural Ireland. A year after her birth, the project was completed, and the family of eleven children moved to Dublin, to a one-room tenement in Mountpleasant Buildings. Because of the dire living conditions in the slum, many of Constance's ten siblings did not make it to adulthood. One respite from the grinding poverty was the residents' own ingenuity in making their own entertainment. Neighbours gathered together in the evenings, sang songs from penny sheets, performed skits for one another and listened through open windows to the street's one wireless (radio) set. It was in this way that Constance received her first training in the dramatic arts. Her father died when she was 15, while she was attending St Louis Convent School in Rathmines. The headstrong teenager gave up school, taking casual jobs as a shop girl and housemaid to support herself. It was this latter position and the encouragement of the owner of the house that set her on the path to stardom. In 1945 she entered a 'Film Star Doubles' contest in *The Screen*, an Irish film-industry publication. She went on to take first place – dressed as Hedy Lamarr in a borrowed dress – at the magazine's ball, attended by local actors, theatre producers and, crucially, international talent scouts. She soon ended up in London and went from there to Hollywood. She was most active in 1950s, appearing in Hollywood features such as *Man in the Attic*, *Treasure of the Golden Condor* and *Impulse*. She was a presenter at the Academy Awards ceremony in 1952. Her last decades were spent, however, dissipated, in and out of hospitals. When able to gather herself together for brief periods, she worked as a cleaner. Constance Smith died in June 2003 in London.

From the 'Highway to Cullenwood' to Mountpleasant Avenue
Behind Mount Pleasant Square, and linked to it, is Mountpleasant Avenue. Many of the houses here also date from the 1830s. Corrigan's Pub dates from the early twentieth century (1910) and around the corner, in the shadow of the impressive green dome of the Church of Our Lady of Refuge, is the picturesque curved line of stucco dwellings known as Bessborough Parade, dating from the 1840s. The avenue was an important route in olden times, linking Aungier and Camden streets to Cullenswood and variously called 'the Milltown Path', 'the Highway to Cullenswood' and the 'Half-Mile Road' since this is the distance between the Canal at Portobello Bridge and Belgrave Square. From the 1830s until the 1860s, house-building continued along this old winding and undulating path, and since it was also the time when the nearby square was being developed, it assumed the name Mountpleasant Avenue. Near Gulistan Avenue, building was diverted because the grounds and boundary of the famous Leinster Cricket Club prevented any such works. This club, founded in 1852, moved to Observatory Lane, its present site, in 1865.

Sunday Evenings with George Russell
One famous resident of this road for a number of years, was George William Russell (1867–1935), who lived at no. 28. He wrote under the pseudonym Æ (signifying the lifelong quest of man), and was a poet, painter, journalist and mystic. He was at the centre of the Irish Literary Revival of the late 1800s and was a supporter of nationalist politics. He was born in Lurgan, Co. Armagh in 1867. His family moved to Dublin in 1878, where he attended a local school in Rathmines. He grew up at Grosvenor Square. He also attended the Metropolitan

School of Art, where he formed a lifelong friendship with the future poet William Butler Yeats. He came to mysticism early on and many of his poems reflect this tendency. In 1897 he became assistant secretary of the Irish Agricultural Organisation Society (IAOS), started by Horace Plunkett in 1894. As a representative of the IAOS, he travelled extensively throughout Ireland, setting up co-operative banks. Though his position in the IAOS prohibited him from expressing political opinions, it was no secret that he was a nationalist. During the 1913 Lockout, he wrote an open letter to *The Irish Times* criticising the employers' actions. Russell was also the editor of several newspapers affiliated with the IAOS, including *The Irish Homestead* (1905–23) and the leading and very influential literary journal *The Irish Statesmen* (1923–30). Throughout his time with the IAOS he continued to write and publish poetry, essays, plays, and novels. He also continued to draw and paint.

Yeats, Joyce and Mary Poppins

Russell was perhaps most important in the way he encouraged young writers, introduced them to useful contacts and acted as a facilitator to the literary renaissance of the time. In 1902 he met a young James Joyce and introduced him to many prominent Irish writers of the day, including Yeats. He appears as a character in the 'Scylla and Charybdis' episode of Joyce's *Ulysses*, where he dismisses Stephen's theories on Shakespeare. Russell was a significant force in Irish cultural life from the 1890s until the 1930s. From 1898, he and his wife Violet held 'at homes' at their house on Mountpleasant Avenue, and later Rathgar Avenue. His Sunday evenings became an important part of the Dublin literary and artistic scene for its leading figures.

   Interestingly, one of the people who was at his bedside when he was dying was Mary Travers (along with Oliver St John Gogarty and Con Curran), the author of *Mary Poppins*! He had published some of her poetry in earlier years and they had maintained a lifelong friendship. He is buried in Mount Jerome Cemetery, Harold's Cross.

Ranelagh's Hidden Gem

Between Ranelagh Road and Mountpleasant Avenue there is a veritable rabbit warren of cottages, two-up two-downs, winding and twisting roads, terraces and avenues, all hidden away from the main roads. Many of the one-storey dwellings date from the early nineteenth century. Names include Bannaville, Mountpleasant Terrace, Ranelagh Mews, Garden View, Athlumney Villas and Mountpleasant Parade. Kelly's

Garage on Bannaville is a family business still thriving after over seventy years. Aidan Kelly retains in his garage an old blue bilingual sign for Mountpleasant Terrace, which spells it with Mount and Pleasant as two separate words. The Gaelic script version is also attractive. In the 1960s the Irish government decided that it would be better if we adopted the English lettering for the Irish language. In one fell swoop, a huge part of our linguistic and cultural heritage was abolished.

When Riverdance Came to Ranelagh

One interesting resident who lived in this little enclave for a number of years was the famous dancer Jean Butler (b. 1971) of *Riverdance* fame. She lived in a very unusual (since its conversion) corner dwelling at no. 9 Mountpleasant Terrace. An American-born step-dancer, choreographer and actress, she is best known for originating the principal female role in the Irish-dance theatrical production *Riverdance*. She began Irish-dance lessons at the age of 6, and in 1994, under the invitation of producer Moya Doherty, she performed in a seven-minute intermission piece at the Eurovision Song Contest, entitled *Riverdance*, a theatrical show consisting mainly of traditional Irish music and dance. The piece was co-choreographed by Butler with Michael Flatley. The riveting performance of both earned a standing ovation from the packed theatre of 3,000 people. In fact, the response was so explosive that shortly afterwards, husband-and-wife production team John McColgan and Moya Doherty expanded it into a stage show, which opened in Dublin on 9 February 1995. Since then, the show has visited over 450 venues worldwide and been seen by over 25 million people, which makes it one of the most successful dance productions in the world. After Flatley left the show in October 1995, Butler was joined by long-time friend Colin Dunne. The pair were the lead dancers when the show played at the famous Radio City Music Hall in New York City. After a long and extremely successful run with the show, Butler eventually left *Riverdance* in January 1997. She retired from active dancing in 2010.

Something you mightn't know is that Butler has appeared in several films: *The Brylcreem Boys*, *Goldfish Memory*, *The Revenger's Tragedy* and *Old Friends*. In January 2011, it was announced that she had designed and released her own jewellery line. The collection was launched at Showcase Ireland at the RDS later that month.

After spending many years living at Mountpleasant Terrace, she later moved to Moyne Road, also in Ranelagh.

7

'THROUGH THE BARRIER PLEASE!' – WATERWAYS, TRAMWAYS AND TRANSPORT

RIVERS AND ROUTES

The Grand Canal, Stout and Turf

The northern boundary of Ranelagh is the Grand Canal waterway. The idea for this canal, which was to link Dublin with the River Shannon, was first mooted in 1715, and construction commenced in the late 1750s with most of it (to Tullamore) completed by 1790. The stretch from Portobello Harbour to Ringsend Basin was started in 1790 and was completed in 1796. The last stretch to the Shannon was finished a few years later, with the official opening in 1804. It was a major means of transport for goods and passengers. The very first trade boat passed from Dublin all the way through to the Shannon in 1804. Typical cargoes on such trade boats would be barrels of Guinness leaving Dublin for rural towns and cargoes of turf coming to Dublin to be burnt in urban fireplaces. The last working cargo barge travelling along the Grand Canal in 1960. Today, it is a popular route for pleasure barges. Moreover, it has traditionally defined the southern boundary of the city centre itself. Today the canal and its banks are an important habitat for wildlife and are used for pleasure boating, walking and cycling in the Ranelagh area. Ranelagh begins at Charlemont Bridge, which crosses the Grand Canal.

The Grand Tour and the Volunteer Earl

Charlemont Bridge, connecting the city to Ranelagh, was called after Charlemont Street, which in turn was named after the Earl of Charlemont. The earl was a general of the Irish Volunteers in the late eighteenth century and a friend of Henry Grattan (of Grattan's parliament). The earl's birthname was James Caulfield and he was born in Dublin in 1728 (d. 1799), the second son of the 3rd Viscount Charlemont, whom he succeeded in 1734. Caulfield, the 1st Earl of Charlemont, definitely left a mark on his native city. At the age of 18, with little formal education, he set off on a Grand Tour of Europe in the company of a teacher, Rev. Edward Murphy. At the time, it was common practice for young men of his class to travel around Europe learning about classical art and history. They certainly took their time, and Caulfield spent nine years visiting Holland, Germany, Italy, Egypt and Greece, where he was particularly impressed by the ancient architecture. He returned to Ireland in 1754, taking his seat in the Irish House of Lords on 7 October of that year. He became known as an Irish statesman with an independent mind, and was created Earl of Charlemont in 1763 for his services in defending Belfast against a possible French invasion. He had commanded the Antrim Volunteers. He opposed the Act of Union of 1800.

Following his return to Dublin, he also decided to build his Casino ('small house') on land he had been given by his stepfather, in Donnycarney. He renamed his estate, Marino, after the small town of Marino, south of Rome. There he built the famous architectural masterpiece, Casino Marino, to plans by Sir William Chambers in 1762. Later, he built a new Charlemont House (now the Dublin City Gallery/the Hugh Lane). He was a founding member and first president of the Royal Irish Academy (RIA), the first session of which convened in his home on 18 April 1785.

The Swan River and Defining Ranelagh

Within walking distance of Charlemont Bridge, the Swan River, although now mainly hidden from view and fitted with culverts, has defined the landscape and topography of Ranelagh. From its source beyond Kimmage Manor, it flows through Rathmines and Ranelagh and then joins the River Dodder at Ballsbridge. In Ranelagh, it flows to the east through Mount Pleasant Square, where the arch leads to Mountpleasant Avenue, before crossing into Ranelagh Gardens. The river was an important factor in the planning and construction of Mount Pleasant Square. Along its journey a number of tributaries are evident. The lake in Ranelagh Gardens is part of the river. At the end of the nineteenth century the Carmelite nuns, now occupying Willsbrook House, complained about the stench of sewage as the river flowed through their grounds. They offered a reward to have culverts put in. The Swan River valley can still be detected in the landscape of the area and is remembered today in the names of Swan Place off Leeson Street,

Swan Grove off Mountpleasant Avenue and both the Swan Centre and Swan Leisure in Rathmines. The river played an important role in delineating boundaries between the c ity and county, between lands and estates and in the building and the shaping of Ranelagh itself. Mount Pleasant Square is an example of this influence as it was designed to take the flow of the nearby river into account.

One of earliest maps of Ranelagh, Taylor's 1816. (Courtesy of UCD Map Library)

TRAINS AND LINES

When one looks at old photographs of Ranelagh in the first decade of the twentieth century there is not a car in sight – truly a joy to behold! Instead, one sees bicycles and horse-drawn carriages, tram poles and lines and maybe a tram trundling along in the distance. By the late 1950s very little had changed except that one might see a few cars cruising gently along. The tram is still to be seen, a modern-day version with a few carriages, but is not an obtrusion and one may, like in those old photos, appreciate the vista of Ranelagh with its different

architectural styles, the shops and even the wide road from the tram. Today, unfortunately, one's appreciation of all that is good and attractive about Ranelagh is often vitiated by the endless lines of cars, the traffic jams, the bottlenecks, cars parked everywhere, and people patiently trying to navigate through the area. But, as I noted above, there was a time when this conundrum did not exist, and the pace of life was more gentle and relaxed. Today, the wheels of commerce go round and round and dictate the frenetic pace of life much in evidence in Ranelagh.

From the Harcourt Street Line to the Green Line

An unusual feature of Ranelagh is the Luas line traversing at the backs of houses, above the main roads and visible in two places near the Triangle. The two bridges are a reminder of the importance of Ranelagh and its role in the development and evolution of the train and light-rail system in Dublin. There was another railway bridge at Dunville Avenue, with the Rathmines and Ranelagh Station under the bridge. This has been replaced by the street-level Beechwood Luas Station. The old Harcourt Street railway line opened in 1854 and ran from Harcourt Street to Bray. The Rathmines and Ranelagh Station on the line opened at Dunville Avenue in 1896. The station was renamed Ranelagh in 1921. With the closure of the line in 1958, the station became obsolete but providentially the structures and alignment of the old line remained mostly intact and it reopened in 2004. This followed the government's decision in 1998 to invest in a new light-rail system in Dublin called

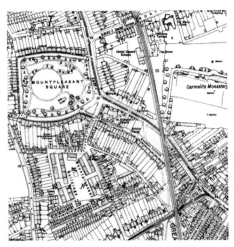

Ranelagh in the early twentieth century with Harcourt Street line slicing through it. (Courtesy of UCD Map Library)

the Luas (Irish word for 'speed'). The Luas Green Line, which opened in 2004, now runs on a large section of the old Harcourt Street line, with stops at Ranelagh and Beechwood. This line serves the south side of Dublin city. It mostly follows the route of the old Harcourt Street railway line, which was reserved for possible reuse when it closed in 1958. In the 1950s, diesel gradually replaced steam in an effort to improve journey times as many passengers had by then forsaken the line due to a rapid and significant increase in private car ownership. CIE were also rapidly expanding their then new bus services in and around the railway. The future of the line looked somewhat bleak.

The Harcourt and the Hilton

Today, between Harcourt Street and Charlemont (over the Grand Canal), the Green Line takes a loop east around buildings, such as the Hilton Hotel and various office buildings, that didn't exist between 1859 and 1959. As such, there is no train bridge on Adelaide Road for the current line, as there had been for the Harcourt Street line. The line then follows the old alignment of the Harcourt Street line from Charlemont as far as Sandyford. There are also some other cosmetic differences between the old line and the new one, such as the positioning of the Ranelagh stop. The location of Ranelagh on the former line was at the current Beechwood stop. The old Ranelagh stop was also the last stop on the old line before the train reached Harcourt Street terminus. The first Luas tram arrived at Beechwood on 30 June 2004.

The Harcourt Street Crash – Through the Buffers

On one occasion, on 14 February 1900, the train from Enniscorthy didn't stop at Harcourt – it kept going through the buffers and the huge grey stone walls of the station until it arrived at Hatch Street on the corner with Harcourt Street, sending debris everywhere. Nobody was killed, though the driver, William Hyland, had his right arm amputated at the scene. Another serious accident occurred on 23 December 1957 when two trains collided in thick fog just south of Dundrum Station. The first train had slowed to a walking pace because of a cow on the line. The second train was allowed into the same section of a track due to an error by a signalman. Its driving cab was completely destroyed in the collision and the driver, Andrew Larkin, was killed instantly.

On the Move – The Nine Arches

One of the major engineering feats on the Harcourt line was the Milltown Viaduct, or Nine Arches, which still stands today over the River Dodder.

Milltown was for many years the site of several working mills on the River Dodder. The spectacular nineteenth-century railway bridge across the river was reopened in 2004 for the Luas light-rail system.

TRAMS AND BUSES

Monsters and 'The Lady of the House'
Besides the train, single-carriage trams, and later buses, were a feature of public transport in Ranelagh and the newer suburbs in the late nineteenth century. The old trams, unlike the modern Luas, used the main roads rather than the railway line. Originally these trams were pulled by horses, but by the end of the nineteenth century, they were electrified.

The poet Katherine Tyan, who lived near the Triangle, recalled with horror the early electric trams. In an article, 'Lady of the House', she remembered going to school in Ranelagh, and it being very near the main road along which the trams passed. She wrote, 'I remember the first trams, monstrous creatures, coming with a creaking and a groaning over Portobello Bridge and hurling themselves like a juggernaut down Richmond Street'. The no. 11 tram used to pass through Ranelagh on its merry way to Clonskeagh where there was a terminus nearly opposite Vergemount Hospital. There was also a Charleston Road line which continued on to Rathmines. This line was later the important part of the no. 18 route. In time, the no. 11 bus took over the tram route through Ranelagh proper. People still recall the early buses pulling in to the bus shelter outside where the Tribeca restaurant is located now. The buses had a driver, up front in his own little cab, while the conductor stood on the platform at the back and banged the bell for the driver either to stop or move off from the bus stop. There was a long silver hand pole at the edge of the platform for passengers to grab hold of when alighting or disembarking. A frequent sight in Dublin at the time was a late passenger rushing after a moving bus and grabbing hold of the bar just in the nick of time and before the bus gathered speed. The reverse was also a common feature, with passengers disembarking as the bus was slowing down. In the process and in order to maintain balance and slow themselves down, passengers appeared to be running after the bus they had just disembarked from! In the bus shelter, there was a clock for the busmen to ensure they stuck to their timetable and they used to 'clock in' with punch cards every time the bus pulled in. You'd know the frequency of buses by the sheer amount of confetti on the ground!

CLOCKS AND TRANSPORT

The 'Correct Time' and the Four-Faced Liar

A reminder today of the importance of the Ranelagh tram route is Tramway Lane, just beyond Sandford Road, on the Clonskeagh Road, nearly opposite Vergemount Hospital. This old lane is beside what was the former terminus building or tram-yard for the trams. Part of the tram-yard is now called Terminus Mills. Speculation has always been rife in Ranelagh and Clonskeagh as to why the terminus was located on the boundary between the two districts and why the tram line did not continue on through Clonskeagh to Goatstown. The answer could well be in the clock perched for decades outside O'Shea's Clonskeagh House. This two-faced old clock, still hanging over an entrance, boldly states 'CORRECT TIME' on its side, for all to see. However, each face of the clock only gives the 'correct time' twice a day and each face gives a different time to the other face. This gave rise to some insurmountable difficulties when the tram drivers and passengers alighted at the terminus building up the hill and around the corner, and quenched their thirst in O'Shea's. Invariably, much later, when they emerged from the establishment, suitably quenched, they noted that despite the time spent inside, according to the clock, they had spent no time at all enjoying themselves! When the Dublin United Tramway Company heard of this they quickly realised that the clock would cause havoc to their timetables if they decided to run the line any further, and so such plans were abandoned and the terminus building remained where it still resides. To this day, the clock continues to confuse the unwary traveller and imbiber!

Ranelagh locals, however, being of an amenable and garrulous disposition generally, and particularly in summer and at Christmas time, regarded the 'correct time' clock as far better than the 'four-faced liar' town hall clock of their Rathmines neighbours. So, if you happen to be passing along Mountpleasant Avenue and glance through the grounds of the Leinster Cricket Club towards the four-faced liar, you will note the time from one face. However, upon arrival onto Rathmines Road, you will probably see the same time displayed again – on one of the clock's four faces anyway!

8

THE DEVIL'S KICK – CHURCHES AND SCHOOLS

PETER, PAUL AND SANDFORD PARISH CHURCH

Sandford Parish Church was designed by Robert Newenham, who lived at nearby Merton House. The land for the church was provided by George Baron Mount Sandford. Newenham had so persuaded Sandford to fund the rebuilding of the church that Sandford later said he acted against the 'Devil's kick'. The new church was built on the same site as a former church which had opened in 1826, but the donated site with extra land enabled a much finer church to be built. In 1860, using some of the original structure, it was rebuilt in the Italian Romanesque style and given a new façade with granite masonry. It was designed by architects Lanyon, Lynn and Lanyon, a Belfast firm, and it was their first Dublin commission. When it officially opened, Sandford became a parish in its own right. The church has a remarkable stained-glass Harry Clarke window, in Art Deco style, dating back to the 1920s. It depicts the saints, Peter and Paul. In front of the church is the attractive one-storey, old lodge, bordering Sandford Road and Merton Road. Behind the church is a hidden gem – Sandford Rectory, a fine house that is practically the same today as it was over 100 years ago. The cross beams extending over the front exterior are a very attractive feature. They are quite similar to the Arts and Crafts architectural style adopted by James Pile with the terrace of houses nearby on Sandford Road, and also to that of Sandford Park House itself, now part of the school complex. All of them date from the close of the nineteenth century and the early twentieth century.

FROM SCULLY'S FIELDS TO BEECHWOOD AVENUE CHURCH

In 1882, the new Parish of the Three Patrons at Rathgar was formed from part of Rathmines, Rathgar, Milltown and the small part of Ranelagh that lay east of Anna Villa. Subsequently the Ranelagh area was part of Rathgar Parish, but with the building of houses and the increasing population towards the end of the nineteenth century, plans were put in place to establish a parish to cater for the area's new needs. A local farmer donated some fields, known as 'Scully's Fields', for the building of a church. While the construction was taking place, a wooden church (known as a chapel of ease), built at Beechwood Avenue in 1898, was used by the parishioners. It was here that 1916 leader Thomas MacDonagh married Muriel Gifford, one of the famous nationalist Gifford sisters from upper Rathmines.

BRASS BANDS, BOYS' BRIGADES AND THE ARCHBISHOP

In 1906, part of Rathgar Parish was detached by drawing a line along part of Dartry Road and part of Palmerston Park and along Palmerston Road, with the lands to the south and east, including Milltown, becoming the new Parish of the Holy Name, Cullenswood. The boundary between the new Cullenswood Parish and the older Rathmines Parish lay along part of Dunville Avenue, Oakley Road, Charleston Road and Ranelagh, thus detaching the area around Beechwood Avenue Lower and Ashfield Road from Rathmines and locating them in Cullenswood. In 1914, when the Church of the Holy Name was formally opened, the new parish, which still included Milltown, had become known as Beechwood Avenue, its formal name today. The Church of the Holy Name was officially opened on 28 June 1914. A contemporary account relates that Archbishop William Walsh 'was met at the end of Beechwood Avenue by a large group of people shortly before 12 o'clock. He was escorted to the church by the Dundrum Brass and Reed Bank and by the Rathmines and Ranelagh Boys' Brigade and the Parish Sodalities', and 'was met at the church by two other bishops and the Parish Priest', who was Fr Thomas Hogan.

THE HARRY CLARKE INFLUENCE

With its dramatic tower and belfry, the church is a striking local landmark. It is very attractive inside, with many mosaics, icons and some interesting stained-glass windows. There are sixty-one window units in the walls of the church. Most are based on traditional interwoven Celtic design in unadorned tinted leaded panes using glass in several shades of blue, brown and green, and in white. It is likely that this design was originally in all the windows of the church with the possible exception of the rose window in the west front. Fifteen of the window units are now glazed in richly stained glass of many colours. It seems possible that all of the glazing at the Church of the Holy Name was carried out by the firm of Joshua Clarke and Sons, whose studios were at 6/7 North Frederick Street, Dublin. This firm changed its name to Harry Clarke Stained Glass Limited in 1930, and continued to operate under that name until 1973, when it closed. Several of the windows with the Celtic design, which it may be assumed were installed before 1921, carry the name of J. Clarke & Sons. Harry Clarke (Henry Patrick Clarke, 1889–1931), who was a son of Joshua Clarke, took over the direction of the firm's stained-glass department in 1921, where, until 1931 when he died, he was inundated with work. Some of the work was made by him, most of it was designed by him and all of it was supervised by him. It is accepted that none of the windows in the Church of the Holy Name were made by Harry Clarke, but it is probable that his hand was involved in their design to some degree.

THE MATT TALBOT CONNECTION

The church seating was probably all installed in the first period and perhaps before the formal opening in 1914. It was made by Messrs T. and C. Martin at their furniture factory on North Wall Quay, Dublin. The famous reformed alcoholic, Matt Talbot, began working in the timber yards of T. and C. Martin in the early 1900s and was employed there continuously until his death in 1925, except for a short break for illness in 1923–24. It is possible then that he was associated with preparing the timber for this seating. The Stations of the Cross in the church were made in November 1913 by Messrs C. Bull, Suffolk Street, Dublin. Austrian and Riga oak was used in the elaborate framing.

ROLLED IN GOLD – FOR WHOM THE BELL TOLLS

There is a dramatic top to the church, comprising a square belfry with a distinctive miniature round-tower feature. There is a viewing area here also. The church belfry contains a stone stairway of 132 steps leading to a flat roof, which commands extensive views across the city and bay, southward to the Dublin and Wicklow Mountains, and westward to open country. The stairway reaches the organ loft in thirty-six steps from the ground floor, and the bell chamber in ninety-six steps. The bell, which has a rim diameter of 1.4 metres (4 feet 8 inches), was originally designed to have the clapper fixed and the bell swinging. On a casting on its east side, it carries the name of its maker, Matthew O'Byrne, Fountain Head Bell Foundry, James' Street, Dublin, and the date 1912. The west side of the bell bears a casting of the crest of Archbishop Walsh (1885–1921) with his motto *Fide et labore*, (faith and labour). There is a persistent oral tradition that gold was incorporated in the metal from which the bell was cast, in order 'to enrich the tone'. The bell is described as being supported by M. Byrne's patent rotary mountings. In recent years, the manual operation of swinging the bell by means of a rope hanging down to the belfry porch has been replaced by an automated electrical system. The local residents are able to hear 'The Bells of the Angelus' as it tolls out twice a day at 12 pm and 6 pm.

THE STEEPLE AND GEORGE BERNARD SHAW – CHRIST CHURCH, LEESON PARK

That towering and impressive structure with a church steeple, Christ Church, is a picturesque landmark situated on the corner of Leeson Street, Dartmouth Road and Leeson Park. It was built to cater for a congregation of 1,200. In its grounds is the Molyneux Asylum for Blind Females which, like the church, was constructed in the years 1860–62. It was built to house 100 females and has an adjoining chapel. Like the church, the asylum is a striking and handsome grey building, in the Tudor Gothic style of plain character, with high-pitched roofs and gables, and dormer and mullioned windows. Granite was the material used, the window and door dressing were chiselled, and the general face of the walls is of hammered stone. The building had three floors.

Between the church and asylum is a commemorative Celtic High Cross for those parishioners of the church who fought and died during the First World War.

Within the space of a few decades from the time of its construction, the church became a Church of Ireland parish catering for the increasing number of members living in the area. One such member was George Bernard Shaw, whose family lived a short stroll away at no. 1 Hatch Street. As a child, he was sent to Sunday school there.

1860 image from Leeson Street of Christ Church, Leeson Park. (Courtesy of the *Dublin Builder*/NLI)

GREAT SCOTT AND JOHN WESLEY

In the closing decades of the twentieth century, the Methodists began to share the church facilities (the Methodist Centenary Church) and later agreed to avail of an old structure, Litton Hall (1877), now part of the Wesley House complex, in the grounds, just beyond the asylum. Its colour and style are in keeping with the church and the asylum and the three buildings complement each other and create a pleasing stairway vista when viewed from Leeson Park. The hall itself was designed by the architect Michael Scott of Bus Áras fame. There is a large carved, circular wall plaque dedicated to the founder of the Methodists, John Wesley, near the hall.

HALLELUJAH! THE CULWICK CHOIR AND THE RYDER CUP

In 1898, the renowned Culwick Choral Society (a mixed choir) began its history in the main church. It was founded by James Culwick, who lived in Leeson Street, and who was a highly respected music teacher. For 118 years, the Culwick has maintained an unbroken tradition of music-making in Dublin. The skill and musicianship of the succession of conductors of the Culwick have been crucial to its success and, from Dr James Culwick onwards, the society has been most fortunate in being led by musicians who could lead a large group of amateur singers to a professional standard of performance. The society has over 100 members drawn from all over Dublin and surrounding counties, and rehearses every Thursday between September and June in Wesley House.

A major choral performance each spring and a concert of seasonal music at Christmas are standard features of the Culwick's busy season. Between 1990 and 2012, a performance of Handel's *Messiah* for charity in St Patrick's Cathedral each winter became an established feature of the Dublin musical calendar. In addition to these activities the choir has also been involved in several events with other choirs, notably Haydn's *Creation* (1998), Verdi's *Requiem* (1999), Dvořák's *Stabat Mater* and Walton's *Belshazzar's Feast* (2004). The society has over the years performed most of the major choral works and has been involved in many Irish premières, including Fanshawe's *African Sanctus*, Bernstein's *Chichester Psalms*, the *Missa Pro Victoria* by Tomás Luis de Victoria and *Return to Old Ireland* (2000) by the modern Irish composer Mary McAuliffe; in 2016, it premiered Roxanna Panafric's *Westminster Mass*.

In 2005, the Culwick was honoured by the Vocal Heritage Association of Ireland at a concert/ceremony in the Bank of Ireland Arts Centre where the choir was privileged to receive the Santa Cecilia Choral Award 2005, a tribute to its founder, Dr James Culwick, and to the choir's contribution to the cultural and civil life in Dublin since its founding in 1898.

In September 2006, the Culwick was chosen as the Ryder Cup Choir to participate in the opening and closing ceremonies of the celebrated golfing tournament at the K-Club in Co. Kildare, and ten years later many of its members participated in 'A Nation's Voice', a 1000-voices strong choir to commemorate the 1916 Easter Rising.

THE MAD MONK AND THE GREEN DOME

A particularly well-known landmark of Ranelagh which is not actually situated in the immediate area is the large and prominent green copper dome of Mary Immaculate, Refuge of Sinners Church on Rathmines Road. This dominates the skyline when viewed from Ranelagh Road and acts as a backdrop to Mount Pleasant Square. The original dome was completely destroyed by fire in 1920 and replaced by the current dome when the church reopened in 1922. The dome, built in Glasgow, Scotland, was destined for a Russian Orthodox church in St Petersburg, but the political and social upheaval there following the two 1917 revolutions, including the Bolshevik Revolution, caused it to be diverted to Dublin. The revolutions witnessed the quick demise of the tsars and of the concomitant influence on the royal family of the infamous Rasputin, known as 'the Mad Monk'. Were it not for the nefarious influence of Rasputin on the tsarina, the skyline of Rathmines and Ranelagh might well have been radically different.

'STICKY FINGERS' BRABAZON AND THE MAGNIFICENT PORTICO

The story of the church itself extends back to 1823 when Dublin's Archbishop Daniel Murray constituted Rathmines as a parish. The land was originally owned by the Brabazon family. The family's connection to Ireland began when William Brabazon was sent to Dublin in the early 1530s by Henry VIII as his vice-treasurer. He was subsequently known as 'Sticky Fingers' Brabazon as a result of his self-aggrandisement at the expense of the Crown. Years later, in 1824, a descendant, the Earl of Meath, sold a plot of land on the border of Rathmines and Ranelagh in 1824 for the building of the church. Lord Brabazon laid the foundation stone. It opened in 1830. Over the succeeding decades, it proved useful but too small for the growing population of Rathmines and Ranelagh. The foundation stone was laid in 1850 and a new church was built to a Byzantine model in the form of a Greek cross. Designed by Patrick Byrne, the church was completed in 1856, with the exception of the portico. This magnificent portico, built from Portland stone, with its four massive columns and their carved Corinthian capitals surmounted by a beautiful pediment, was completed twenty-five years later. Everything was well until a tragic fire in 1920 which saw the dome collapse, crashing to the ground with a sound that was heard for miles around. Reconstruction of the church began immediately and the church reopened after five months. The outstanding feature of the reconstructed building was the dome, visible from a distance, including from the Dublin Mountains.

SANDFORD PARK SCHOOL AND WILLIAM TREVOR

Sandford Park School, a co-educational private school, is situated in and around James Pile's former and very distinctive house, built in 1894. The house had an ornamental pond and island, a sunken tennis court, a mews yard, and a ballroom complete with a minstrel's gallery. Great care had been lavished on the building of this house, which has panelled rooms and ornate ceilings. The school took up residency there in 1922, having moved from Earlsfort Terrace. It is surrounded by 2.5 hectares of secluded and beautifully wooded grounds, replete with sports pitches and games facilities. Interestingly, its first headmaster, Alfred Le Peton, had no formal qualifications for his role. He, however, had a strong philosophy with regard to education: the young had to take 'responsibility for their own lives' and the role of the educator was 'to provide opportunities and the motivation to bring about this desired end'. As well as this independence of spirit and individualism, he believed in the importance of having a strong sense of 'community' or *esprit de corps*. One of the school's most illustrious pupils was the great Irish novelist William Trevor, who later recalled being bashed up by the prefects, as was the norm in the school at the time.

LOUISE GAVAN DUFFY, THE GPO AND SCOIL BHRÍDE

Louise Gavan Duffy, born in France in 1884, was the daughter of Sir Charles Gavan Duffy, Young Irelander and founder and editor of *The Nation* newspaper. He had lived in Ranelagh at various times during his career. Louise's brother was George Gavan Duffy, one of the plenipotentiaries sent to negotiate with the British government in 1921 during the War of Independence. He was subsequently one of the five signatories of the Treaty that was the outcome of the negotiations. He was later minister for foreign affairs in the First Dáil and, still later, president of the High Court. Louise Gavan Duffy came to live in Ireland in 1907 and studied the Irish language both in Dublin and in the Gaeltacht and then trained to be a teacher. She taught for a time at Pearse's new experimental school for girls, Scoil Íde at Cullenswood House, Ranelagh. Pearse's objective was to attempt for Irish girls what had been so successfully achieved for Irish boys at St Enda's College in Rathfarnham. The staff also included the writer and critic Mary Maguire, who would later marry Longford poet Padraic Colum. Willy Pearse was the art master.

THE 1916 RISING – HELPING OUT IN THE GPO KITCHENS

When Scoil Íde closed in 1912, Louise became a member of Cumann na mBan and her detailed statement to the Bureau of Military History describes her journey through Dublin on Easter Monday 1916, and her arrival at the GPO, where she asked to see Pearse: 'I said to him that I wanted to be in the field but that I felt that the Rebellion was a frightful mistake, that it could not possibly succeed, and that it was, therefore, wrong.' Pearse suggested that she help out in the kitchens, and she agreed to this, since it was not active service. She stayed there until the GPO was evacuated on Friday, and next morning went to Jacob's 'to see what they were going to do there'. Following the 1916 Rising, Louise Gavan Duffy went on to establish Scoil Bhríde in 1917. This was Ireland's first Gaelscoil for girls, based on the principles established in Scoil Íde. The school was located on St Stephen's Green, then it moved to Earlsfort Terrace and later to Oakley Road. This was to be her main life's work until her death in 1969. Today, the school continues to thrive and some say that it is the school of choice for the sophisticated élite in the surrounding suburbs who have belatedly awakened, embraced ownership and become comfortable (to some degree) with their unique cultural heritage, though this does not involve sacrificing a worldly vision either. In 1997, to cater for the demand, another school was opened in Cullenswood House, Lios na nÓg. In 1979 there were twenty-five Gaelscoilleanna in Ireland; today there are more than 200, with numbers rising rapidly. Louise Gavan Duffy was instrumental in that success.

FROM COFFEE MAKING TO NOTE TAKING – GONZAGA COLLEGE

The property on which Gonzaga College was built, including two fine houses, Sandford Hill and Sandford Grove, and surrounding lands of about 15 acres, was purchased by the Jesuits in 1949 from the Bewley family. The intention was to open a preparatory school here. The houses are now part of the Gonzaga College complex. The purchased properties are adjacent to lands already owned by the Jesuits in Milltown Park. The first rector of the new school was Fr Charles O'Connor, known as 'the O'Connor Don'.

COLLEGE OF INDUSTRIAL RELATIONS

Sandford Lodge, a property also in the acquired grounds, became the headquarters of Catholic Workers' College, an industrial-relations initiative established in the early 1950s under the auspices of the Jesuits to try and reconcile workers' and employers' differences and problems through the process of teaching about rights and obligations. The Jesuits hoped that the college would develop, through education, leadership in workplaces and trade unions. The first course for trade unionists began in 1951. It subsequently evolved into the College of Industrial Relations and now the National College of Ireland, having moved in recent years to the International Financial Services Centre in Dublin 1.

SANDFORD PARK CO-EDUCATIONAL SCHOOL – FROM HOME TO SCHOOL

George Sandford, a generous benefactor, besides financing Sandford Park Church, also donated property for Sandford National School and for what subsequently became a girls' secondary school and latterly a co-educational school. The house, Sandford House, a most impressive structure, was built by James Pile in 1894 and is a larger version of some of the similar mock-Tudor houses he built nearby on Sandford Road. It is still *in situ*.

ALDO ROSSI, RICHNESS OF DIVERSITY AND THE RMDS

The Ranelagh Multi-Denominational School (RMDS), established in September 1988, is located on the main Ranelagh Road close to the Luas station and Mount Pleasant Square. It is on the site of the old St Columba's National School, which was donated to RMDS by the Church of Ireland. This was known as the 'tin school' and was built in 1893. It was decided to demolish the old and begin afresh. The new school – the RIAI Gold Medal award-winning RMDS – was designed by O'Donnell & Tuomey Architects and opened in 1998. It was subsequently extended. The new building is contemporary in design but its scale and finishes (salvaged yellow bricks and timber) are in sympathy with the area's historic buildings. The school was built in consultation with local residents and conservation groups and the eventual choice of brickwork was deliberate to ensure this new structure would complement the colour and character of neighbouring properties and in particular Mount Pleasant Square. The old and the new spoke to each other, as it were, an architectural principle espoused in particular by the Italian architect Aldo Rossi, who was also an inspiration for the Group '91 architects that included O'Donnell & Tuomey Architects, working on the rejuvenation of Temple Bar from the early 1990s onwards. The RMDS was originally an eight-classroom school but was subsequently extended, reflecting its popularity and the growing community in the immediate vicinity. Its philosophy underpins its teaching – 'That every person is entitled to equal respect regardless of age, gender, nationality, religious beliefs, social and cultural background or economic status'. The school won many awards for the eye-catching architecture of the building. It was cited as the best building completed in Ireland toward the close of the twentieth century.

9

PARKS, PUNDITS AND SPORT

PARKS AND PERSONALITIES

From Pleasure Gardens to Piety

Ranelagh Gardens is a hidden treasure of a park located behind the houses and shops of Ranelagh. Unless one knows of its existence, in fact, it is quite easily overlooked, as it is not visible from the main road. Yet, there is an impressive entrance under the Luas bridge and through the former high gates of the old convent. In 1768 a businessman, William Hollister, took the lease on Willbrook House and set in train plans to open the Ranelagh Pleasure Gardens as a place of entertainment for the well-to-do of Dublin. Within a few years, the 5 hectares of pleasure gardens were developed in the grounds of Willbrook House, and called after Lord Ranelagh of Co. Wicklow, who had similar pleasure gardens in London. These were beside the site that now hosts the Chelsea Flower Show. The current park, owned by Dublin City Council, extends to 1 hectare, with the rest developed for houses and apartments. The design of the park includes an ornamental pool, thereby restoring the historical connection. Today, some of the old trees from the original estate are still present and the pond is also a reminder of the laying-out of the Ranelagh Gardens. There is also a memorial statue to one Richard Crosbie and a memorial cross to another former tenant of nearly 200 years – the Carmelite Nuns.

Brambles, Bites and the Not-so-blind Bats

An old gate lodge beside the Ranelagh Road entrance is an impressive sight as one enters the park. Oftentimes, Harry the Heron is sighted, perched upon the chimney pots. Harry the Heron is a reminder that parks like Ranelagh Gardens are important for wildlife as the lines of trees and hedgerows provide continuous corridors in which wildlife travels, shelters and feeds. Native plants found in the park, such as bramble, ivy and willow, provide food for wildlife by producing fruit and by attracting more insects than non-native species.

The long pond, grassland, shrubs and trees offer much-needed refuge for flora and fauna in the city. The pond supports a spawning population of carp on an annual basis. It is also an important city habitat for insects, which need waterbodies for stages in their life cycles. These insects in turn provide food for bats and birds. The island in the pond attracts waterbirds, including the mute swan, tufted duck and mallard, which nest and rear their young here. Bats, the only mammal capable of true flight, are one of the more remarkable species found in the park. There are ten species of bats in Ireland and eight of these can be found in Dublin. These are highly protected animals and, despite common myths, they are not blind. They can see as well as humans and don't fly into your hair. Bats use echolocation to feed on insects at night by making high-pitched squeaks and listening for echoes that bounce off their prey. This benefits humans as some of the insects are species that bite.

The Aeronautic Chariot or Flying Barge

The park became part of aviation history when Richard Crosbie (1755–1824) became the pilot of the first manned balloon flight in Ireland on 19 January 1785. On that day at 2.30 pm, Crosbie launched, from an exhibition area at Ranelagh Gardens, his grand air balloon and flying barge, in which he intended to cross the Irish Sea. Earlier, in 1784, Crosbie had exhibited his 'aeronautic chariot' at Ranelagh Gardens. Made of wood covered with cloth, designed and built by himself, the chariot resembled a boat, with rudder and sails, intended to enable navigation in the air, reducing reliance on wind direction. It came shortly (fourteen months) after the invention of the hot-air balloon by the Montgolfier brothers, which resulted in the first manned flight in 1783 at Versailles in France. Their inspiration came from one of the brothers observing laundry as it dried over a fire forming pockets that billowed upwards.

Crosbie was 6 feet 3 inches tall and from Crosbie Park near Baltinglass in Wicklow. He had launched several balloons containing animals, such as cats, before attempting the first human flight on Irish soil. At the time, Crosbie was regarded in the same way astronauts were in the twentieth century. His was an attempt to conquer the sky. There was much public excitement and international publicity consequently. Crosbie's first flight took place on 19 January 1785 at Ranelagh and was witnessed by more than 35,000 people. The balloon and 'chariot' were beautifully painted with the arms of Ireland supported by images of Minerva and Mercury, and with emblematic figures of the wind. According to the *Limerick City Journal*, Crosbie's aerial dress 'consisted of a robe of oiled silk, lined with white fur, his waistcoat and breeches in one, of white satin quilted, and morocco boots, and a montero cap of leopard skin'. He had defied a ban on balloon flights by the Lord Mayor of Dublin, which had been put into effect because the population of the city was spending long periods gaping at the sky instead of working. Crosbie's hydrogen air balloon ascended skywards from the Ranelagh Gardens in the first manned balloon flight in Ireland, thereby making aviation history. He was 30 at the time and hoped to cross the Irish Sea. However, darkness and wintry weather conditions forced the balloon to land on Clontarf strand in north County Dublin. Crosbie was rescued by the Dun Laoghaire barge *Captain Walmitt*, which was following his progress.

In 1787 Hollister closed the gardens as interest waned and the public's attention was distracted by other delights, including the Rotunda Gardens across the River Liffey, St Stephen's Green and the other fine Georgian squares springing up around Dublin.

Stamps and the Statues

Two hundred years later, An Post celebrated the historic event with two stamps. On 28 September 2008, in Ranelagh Gardens, in conjunction with the Ranelagh Arts Festival, Councillor Mary Freehill, on behalf of the lord mayor, unveiled a sculpture to commemorate Richard Crosbie, 'the first Irishman to fly', often called 'the father of Irish aviation'. His achievement was being commemorated by a memorial close to the original site of the historic event. The statue, which was designed by leading Irish artist Rory Breslin, depicts Richard Crosbie's youthful curiosity and many of the items displayed on the bronze reflect an airborne theme. The sculpture, which is adorned with various images, gives a sense of the showmanship, extravagance and ornamentation that were evident on the actual day in January 1785. It is designed to be a fitting commemoration to Richard Crosbie and his redoubtable curiosity and determination while also being a timeless piece of art in its own right. According to Terry Connaughton of the Ranelagh Arts Centre, the statue 'is both a symbol of the resurgence of the cultural life of Ranelagh Village and a fulcrum point of the ever-popular walks and talks that are a feature of the annual Ranelagh Arts Festival'.

Playing to the Madding Crowd – The Dillon Garden

For many years, secreted behind the quiet façade of the handsome Georgian terraced house at 45 Sandford Road (also Sandford Terrace), there was a truly inspirational garden. It was long hailed as 'the best garden in Dublin' and was developed over the decades by Helen Dillon, one of Ireland's most highly regarded gardeners. She valued the half-acre garden for its beauty, the therapeutic effect, and the curiosity it aroused. It became celebrated around the world for its exuberant displays of perennials grouped around an elegant formal water feature based on a Moorish fountain and canal. They included tender and hardy plants from five continents, grouped in exotic and colourful combinations. Dillon was also a columnist, and one of her columns was called 'Near to the Madding Crowd'. She firmly believed that gardens must always 'move on', that unlike pictures they are forever changing. Yet she never regarded looking after a garden as 'work'. 'Playing', she called it. Thousands of people visited this fantastic garden from the time it was first opened around 1990. One of those visitors was Robin Lane Fox, the gardening columnist with the *Financial Times*. He was also bowled over and described it as 'the best walled town garden one can hope to see'. 'The lilies are stupendous, the colours of the crocosmias far brighter than mine and the glaucous-leaved cannas are a revelation. It looks at the moment like a bowl of smarties – the effect is stunning.' There was much more, including the alpine house, the conservatory, the clumps of angel's fishing rods arching over sphinxes and *Lapageria rosea* – the national flower of Chile, regarded as a most beautiful climber. The borders were packed with unusual and exotic plants, shrubs, colourful flowers, including lady's slipper orchids – a veritable feast of colour, beauty and aromas. Consequently, and justifiably, with all its saturated hues, the garden was one of the most talked-about in Ireland.

Stones, Roses and the Queen of Irish Gardening

Helen Dillon was long renowned as the 'queen of Irish gardening'. According to Helen's husband, Val, when they first started working on the garden it was full of weeds and they had to use a dinner fork to dig them out! For him, 'grass was a pain in the ass', and later they had the fine lawn replaced with an elongated lake and Irish limestone paving. Its inspiration came from the Alhambra in Spain and the central canal in the palace's Court of Myrtles. One of the many visitors to the garden was The Rolling Stones' Mick Jagger, who cut a record in Dublin at the time. He was so taken by the house and garden that he rented it from the owners for a few weeks while staying in Dublin. Many years later, in 2016, the Dillons took the decision to downsize and sell the house and garden. The glorious twenty-five-year period during which it was open to the public sadly came to an end. People, like gardens, change and move. In the year the garden closed its gates for the last time, celebrated garden-writer Helen Dillon hung up her secateurs and left her Dublin home after forty-four happy years.

The Sandford Road Medicine Man

In the National Botanic Gardens in Glasnevin, there is a portrait of a renowned botanist, one Augustine Henry (b. Co. Derry, 1857–1930), dating from 1929. The National Library of Ireland also have a photograph of him dating from the early 1920s and he is shown, with his wife, in the company of Sir Jocelyn Gore Booth, surrounded by trees, at Lissadell House in Co. Sligo. By sheer coincidence this medical doctor, plantsman and sinologist lived next door from what later became the Dillon Garden. He lived at no. 5 Sandford Terrace (now no. 47 Sandford Road) and yet spent many years of his life in China investigating plant life and studying the plants used in Chinese medicine. From there he sent to the Royal Botanic Gardens or Kew Gardens, in Richmond, Surrey, thousands of samples, seeds, saplings and every imaginable specimen of the exotic plants he came across. When he returned to Kew Gardens, he became interested in trees and was the joint author (with J.H. Elwes) of a seven-volume *Trees of Great Britain and Ireland*, a massive undertaking and achievement.

East Meets West in the National Botanic Gardens

It was originally published in *c*. 1913 and was reprinted in 2014 by Cambridge University Press. It was said that Henry's work in the East beautified the gardens of the West. In 1913, he also took up a post in Dublin as professor of forestry at the Royal College of Science (now part of the National University of Ireland), saying that he would like to do some work for his own country. At the time of his death, he had a private collection of over 10,000 specimens, which his wife had catalogued and then donated to the National Botanic Gardens as the Augustine Henry Forestry Herbarium. He is regarded as the founding father of Irish forestry. Years later, in the Dillon Garden next door, there was a reminder and acknowledgement of him, with the *Lilium Henryi*.

The Pleasant Little Park

In recent years, the small and curving L-shaped park between the tennis courts of Mount Pleasant Square and Ranelagh Road has been renovated and decorated. Sited at the entrance to Ranelagh Village, with the curved terraces surrounding it, the original park, minus the tennis club with its courts, dates from 1848 and was called Mount Pleasant Square Park. Over time and with the opening of the tennis club, the much-reduced park gradually became unkempt and unused. In stepped the nearby Ranelagh multi-denominational school and the Mount Pleasant Square Residents' Association. They recognised its potential and successfully lobbied the Dublin City Council to have it replanted and revitalised. Now it is a delight and is much used, and even hosts the Ranelagh Dog Show. An interesting feature of the new park is an embedded line, hammered into Wicklow granite slabs, that follows the subterranean course of the Swan River. It was also quite fortuitous that, coincidentally, a local resident and Dublin City Council architect, Susan Roundtree, had an input into the impressive project.

THE SPORTING LIFE IN RANELAGH

Mount Pleasant and Fitzwilliam LTCs

It must be interesting for Ranelagh resident and renowned soccer pundit Eamon Dunphy to hear, day-in day-out, the constant sound of tennis balls being swatted back and forth. Mount Pleasant LTC was founded in 1893, which makes it one of the oldest clubs in the city. The family of the developer who built the surrounding square was much involved in the club and Henry Joseph Dolan was its first president. The logo of the club includes a swan in its centre, thereby giving recognition to the nearby Swan River (now fitted with culverts), as well as to the many swans that are a near-permanent feature of the Grand Canal. It is the only club in the city which has squash, tennis and badminton sections. It holds the annual Tennis Open Week, one of the largest tournaments in Ireland. For years, the Pavilion was also a popular venue for 'dances'. One cannot fail, however, to notice nearly twenty massive arc lights towering into the sky and obliterating any view of the square itself, an eyesore compounded by an obtrusive pavilion. Saying that, it is nonetheless a tremendous asset to the upwards of 1,000 members who use its facilities.

Despite this being one of the oldest clubs in the city, there is an even older club on the fringes of Ranelagh at Winton Road and the Appian Way – the Fitzwilliam Lawn Tennis Club. This was established in 1877, which made it one of the oldest tennis clubs in the world. However, it is, unlike Mount Pleasant LTC, a private-members club. It did not move to its present location until 1969.

Gael Force in Ranelagh

Going by the clientele in some pubs in Ranelagh at certain times of the year, it is reasonable to say that the area seems to attract 'rugby types', if there is such a class. This is not surprising, given the interest of some residents in the area, its close proximity to Aviva and the rugby clubs in the Dublin 4 vicinity, and the fact that local schools such as Gonzaga don't exactly encourage Irish national games. Moreover, there aren't too many areas in the country that have roads like those in Ranelagh, called Rugby Road and Rugby Villas.

Despite that, and maybe because of it, the GAA gets a good look-in and has made its presence felt in Ranelagh in a very positive way. The initiative was taken in 2003, when a few locals, led by the vision of Liam O'Hagan, decided to start a GAA club in the village and that year Ranelagh Gaels was born with just one team playing challenge matches around the county. They grew from there and the club recently topped a league in the Dublin County Championship. They play their home games in Bushy Park in Terenure, and train in UCD. In 2006, the Gaels reached a first championship final, losing to a strong St Vincent's side at Parnell Park. Ranelagh's first silverware was secured in 2007, the O Broin Cup, and in 2008 and '09 back-to-back promotions were secured. The year 2009 was a landmark in more ways than one, with a ladies' team established, which competed in the league in 2010 and spectacularly won the Dublin Junior E Championship in the same year. In 2015, Ranelagh Gaels fielded the club's first hurling team at underage and the ladies were awarded the Division 5 Cup after a thrilling win over Foxrock-Cabinteely. The club also has the popular Ranelagh Gaels Juvenile Academy, offering local youngsters an opportunity to represent their area on the playing fields of Dublin. The Dick Morrissey Cup, called after a founder member of the club, and provided by his family, was unveiled at a special ceremony in Birchall's Pub. Dick Morrissey was there from the very start and he went on to serve as chairman and president of the club, a position he held at the time of his death in 2012. Ranelagh Gaels is a classic example of the adage 'from small acorns great oak trees grow' and it has grown to be a permanent fixture in the area.

If one finds tennis or Gaelic football too strenuous, the opportunities to practise yoga abound with the Raja Yoga Centre on Leeson Park and Yoga Dublin Studios on Dartmouth Place. Alternatively, you might just like to go for a walk in Ranelagh Gardens.

The Fab Four and the Rovers of Milltown

The area is still associated with the famous Shamrock Rovers Football Club, which played just around the corner from Sandford Road and Milltown Park at Glenmalure Park. The football grounds were on land leased from the Jesuits. The famous club was based here from 1926 until 1987 when it was controversially sold for house building. The 1920s was a very successful time for Rovers. The club won the title in their very first season as members of the League of Ireland, scoring an all-time record of seventy-seven goals and suffering just one defeat in the process. By now Rovers had secured their own ground on the Milltown Road, which was only a short walk from their support base of Ringsend-Irishtown-Sandymount. The title came to Milltown again in 1924/25 when they also won the FAI Cup, having beaten rivals Shelbourne 2–1 at Dalymount Park before 25,000 spectators. The emergence of the famous 'Four Fs' in the Rovers forward line, Fullam, Fagan, Farrell and Flood, was to capture the public imagination. Crowds of up to 30,000 were often recorded for the big games. Rovers soon became known as the 'cup specialists' as they captured the FAI Cup five years in a row from 1929 to 1933. It was in 1931/32 that they had won their second double. At this time, players such as Bob Fullam, David 'Babby' Byrne, William 'Sacky' Glen, Dinny Doyle and Charlie Jordan were all household names.

Paddy Coad and 'The Hoops'

It was in 1927 that Rovers first donned the green-and-white hooped jerseys and soon earned themselves the nickname of 'the Hoops'. A new record was set in 1945 when Rovers beat Bohemians in the FAI Cup with an all-time high attendance of 41,238. It was in 1942 that an inside forward by the name of Paddy Coad was to join the club from Waterford. At the time, nobody could have envisaged the impact that Coad was to have on the club. He was to win every honour in the game including eleven international caps, and he was to captain the Hoops to unprecedented success in the next decade. With the untimely death of Jimmy Dunne in November 1949, Coad reluctantly accepted the offer by the owners of the club, the Cunningham family, to take over Dunne's role. He brought many young players into the team and by the time Rovers won the League title in 1953/54 he had put together what many old supporters now believe to have been the best Hoops team ever. They went on to win the League in 1956/57 and 1958/59 as well as the FAI Cup in 1955 and 1956. Many other honours in the shield and various cup competitions were also won. Almost all of the players who donned the green and white became international players, including Eamon Darcy, Ronnie Nolan, Shay Keogh, Gerry Mackey, 'Maxie' McCann, Liam Tuohy, Paddy Ambrose, Tommy Hamilton, Noel Peyton and of course Coad himself. Two other famous personalities associated with

Shamrock Rovers were Johnny Giles and Eamon Dunphy, the latter later returning to his football roots and living in Ranelagh.

The Pundit and Ranelagh – 'You have to be a bastard!'

Eamon Dunphy, Irish media personality, broadcaster, journalist, author, sports pundit and former professional footballer, lives in Ranelagh to this day. In recent years he has, with equally legendary footballers Johnny Giles and Liam Brady, entertained huge audiences anxious to watch and listen to their RTÉ match commentary. For Eamon Dunphy, a legend to this day, football and controversy go hand-in-hand. He has much experience, having played professional football for a number of teams, including Millwall and Shamrock Rovers, and having made twenty-three appearances with the Irish national team. So, he knows the game from the inside and this comes across vividly when he gives his views on RTÉ, in his columns or in interviews. In the process, his and our emotions are in turmoil. Our sympathies, our hatreds, deepest antagonisms and passions are tossed backwards and forwards, up and down the field of play, till we eventually feel we have had our heads knocked about – in a happy sense. Why? His angry love for the game is palpable, visceral, challenging and essential for a real appreciation of the beautiful game. For Mr Dunphy tells it as it is, or as *he* sees it. For instance, he told his friend, fellow Ranelagh sportsman Ken Doherty, that he, Ken, was 'too f...ing nice. You have to be a horrible bastard', if you want to win. That is his style – upfront with the facts, whether you like it or not. As recently as 2017, he agreed with the decision that the Leicester manager should be sacked, despite that team (rank outsiders) having won the Premier League in May 2016, thereby creating football history. 'If it had been my club, I'd have done the same. This is a business,' he said. 'It's not like an amateur sport.' Total honesty to readers, viewers and listeners where honesty is still a novelty. He regarded himself 'as a good player, not a great player'. Despite his modesty, he remains truly a legend, a great legend. He has enriched our lives immeasurably.

10

FROM THE PARLOUR TO PINOCCHIO – FOOD GLORIOUS FOOD

PARADISE – MORELLI'S AND THE PRONTO

In the 1950s, there were at least ten grocers, newsagents and tobacconists and five hardware shops in Ranelagh. One such well-known newsagents was Keighron's, which survived until the early years of the twenty-first century. Many have been replaced by a few big supermarkets, such as Spar, Supervalu and Lidl. Most of the small family businesses have long disappeared. The premises are still there but with different tenants, reflecting the changed social mores, attitudes and lifestyles of the local population. Now, many of these former local shops, often family-run businesses, are occupied by restaurants and sundry cafés/takeaways. Today, the main thoroughfare through the village has been transmogrified into the food paradise that is Ranelagh, with at least forty restaurants and pubs. This breaks down to approximately thirty-five restaurants/cafés/takeaways and six pubs.

For many years, there were only a few places to eat in what are nowadays called 'takeaways', but were previously called 'chippers'. Some might recall the Pronto Grill (now Tribeca) or the Paradise Grill, and Morelli's Chip Shop (where Antica Venezia, established in 1998, is now located). The latter was often regarded as the centre of the universe for some of the young locals. There they could smell and taste the sizzling chips, drink their black Coke or Pepsi, and listen to the latest pop music on the jukebox. At the opposite end of the spectrum, McCambridge's and Redmond's have long been associated with good food and fine wines. Except for Redmond's, all the old hands have gone since Ranelagh became one of the most desirable areas to live in and today the village's upmarket residential hinterland feeds into the vibrant restaurant and bar trade at its centre.

THE CRANKY CRITIC AND THE VIRTUOUS TART

When it comes to food and restaurants, it can only help to have the 'super foodie' Susan Jane White living in Ranelagh. She is also married to a 'cranky' restaurant critic. She calls herself a 'nutritional cook or "nut" for short!' Seemingly, when she was involved in the Oxford Gastronomy Society, she weaned an entire generation of students off antidepressants, M&Ms and dodgy kebabs. Years later, her cookbooks have a cult following which, according to herself, 'allows her to misbehave regularly on radio and TV'. Her book *The Extra Virgin Kitchen* was a best-seller and a more recent book, *The Virtuous Tart*, won the Cookbook of the Year Award. She was also involved in a campaign with another local, football pundit Eamon Dunphy, to protect Cullen's corner shop at the junction of Lower Mountpleasant Avenue and Richmond Hill.

THE MINT AND THE PRESSURE COOKER

Of course, mention has to be given to 'chef of chefs' Dylan McGrath and the Mint Restaurant, which was located in the heart of Ranelagh for a number of years in the first decade of the twenty-first century. This wasn't just any kind of restaurant – it was a Michelin star-winning restaurant owned by the controversial celebrity chef. The restaurant featured in the 2008 RTÉ fly-on-the-wall documentary *The Pressure Cooker*. The programme led to some complaints from his fellow chefs about his alleged less-than-sensitive treatment of his staff, which often involved raising his voice. Despite that, *Image* magazine described Mint as 'a place of worship' and *Hot Press* magazine called the venue a 'gastronomic playground'. The praise didn't stop there as Ross Bannon of the *Sunday Business Post* added his memorable line, 'It is a long time since a meal actually haunted me in a way that a beautiful painting or a thoughtful book might'. The *Irish Independent*, not to be outdone, described Mint 'as one of the sublime places to enjoy cutting-edge contemporary cooking'. The high-calibre restaurant thrived until April 2009 when, alas, the effects of the economic recession took their toll

Grumpy Mule tea and coffee is particularly appropriate for those seeking such a cure. They also provide 'calorie-counted menus', which are very useful for those with a hangover, trying to come to their senses while enjoying the 'jumbo' or 'ranch style' breakfast.

After breakfast, you may well be thinking of lunch. All is well, as La Réserve Brasserie will meet your needs. They call themselves 'an intimate and lively French artisan brasserie' and they provide a 'market menu', including a 'lunchbox special so you can return to work quickly'. The speciality here is 'French classics with influences from international cuisine' underpinned by 'authentic and exceptional flavours'.

THE TASTE OF MUSIC – FROM EDELWEISS TO EDELWISE

A few doors along we have Edelwise, another 'authentic' experience, this time of Swiss food and wine culture. Edelweiss itself is a white flower found high in the Swiss Alps and the name came to prominence in a 1959 Rodgers and Hammerstein musical (later film), *The Sound of Music*. In the musical, 'Edelweiss', the song, was sung as a statement of Austrian patriotism in the face of the Nazi advance. The flower (also grown in Austria) was seen as a symbol of loyalty to Austria. Today it may be seen on the Austrian 2 cent euro coin.

Beetroot risotto would be an interesting try in Edelwise. Its 'Petite Arvine' has been described as 'weighty, textured and quite delicious'. It was said that its fondue, a Swiss dish of melted cheese served in a communal hot pot, e.g. *moitié-moitié* four-cheese fondue with veg, would 'create a good mood'. The first-known recipe, from the mid-1870s, was with cheese and wine, no eggs. In the 1930s it was promoted as a Swiss national dish by the Swiss Cheese Union, but over time its meaning has evolved to include chocolate fondue and other dishes, with the approach being to dip food into a shared pot of hot liquid. Today, cheese fondue consists of a blend of cheeses, wine and seasoning, and diners dip bread speared on a fondue fork into the mixture.

ATTITUDE AND ALCATRAZ

When one thinks of Dillinger's, further along the Ranelagh strip, the name John Dillinger, an American gangster from the Depression era, comes to mind. Today, Dylan McGrath's former Mint restaurant has been commandeered and called Dillinger's. Keeping with the American theme, Dillinger's take this Dillinger legacy and attitude very seriously – 'a knife, a fork, a bottle and a cork, that's the way we spell New York ...'. Their 'American-influenced progressive food is not precious, but proud', they insist. To emphasise, 'it's fun, punchy, generous and all about flavour and integrity'. Sounds very like something Mr Dillinger himself might say. The décor of Dillinger's is like that of the set for *The Maltese Falcon*. Moreover, they clearly spell out what's in store for 'fiends' – Margarita Mondays, Nacho Tuesdays, Steak Wednesday – it sounds like the menu in Alcatraz. A caveat, however – you may also eat 'Norwegian eggs' and 'elderberry juice'. That the eggs, insisted a waiter, 'were to die for', would also resonate with Mr Dillinger.

Milano's and Mario's on opposite sides near the Triangle offer Italian fare. Mario's has been in business in Ranelagh for nigh on twenty-five years, with many of the same staff providing consistently excellent pizzas, pasta, lasagne and much more.

ATTITUDE AND AVOCADOS

From 'smashed avocados' to 'crushed avocados' – this is one's choice in Ranelagh. Brioche, on the corner of Elmwood Avenue, offers the latter. But they also offer '48-hour cured salmon' and, if you are so inclined, 'chicken and egg'. They don't spell out which comes first, however, but that's perfectly acceptable since there is an emphasis on 'casual'. In any case, in an industry full of noise, they are 'champions of local Irish produce' and allow the fruit of their labour do the talking. Paolo Tullio, food critic of the *Irish Independent*, was of the view that 'each one of these dishes was perfectly executed and a couple were truly exceptional'. Many other discerning diners added their praise: 'the cooking shows real pedigree', said one, and Catherine Cleary, food critic of *The Irish Times*, went even further – 'Brioche is wowing Ranelagh residents, no mean feat in this restaurant-heavy village'.

CUPCAKES AND IRISH COOKING

Gammells, with its inviting and colourful-looking window, situated on the corner with the Triangle, combines a bakery, delicatessen and patisserie. Its eye-catching window glows with a full array of treats and cakes concurring with the season or celebration. Here you will enjoy a display of cake stands, a flurry of bows and whatever else it takes to add to the novelty. You will even see 'Sex in the City cupcakes' in the window at various times, with vibrantly coloured in deep pinks, electric blues, or bright blues. Gammells has an interesting pedigree. The bakery originates from its long connection with the McCambridge's brown soda bread family who had operated in the building next door to the present Gemmells. Consequently, the standard is very high. In the McCambridge's era, bakeries of that calibre were infrequent. 'Gourmet' was not just an exotic word in its case. McCambridge's was a feature of Ranelagh. Luckily, the tradition continues with Gammells. The name comes from Brendan Gammell, a former manager of McCambridge's, who opened his own business in the 1980s when McCambridge's closed the bakery and shop and concentrated their efforts elsewhere. He knows all about tradition, quality and standards and his customers return time and time again to savour Irish cooking at its best.

FROM POTSTICKERS TO WALLS OF NUT BUTTER

Around the corner from Gammells and skirting the Triangle, various restaurants, cafés and takeaways seem to regularly pop up and then, after a suitable interlude, disappear. Godfather's Pizza is gone, as is the Chinese restaurant. However, Wow Burger has taken up tenancy and here you will be able to sample 'thick shakes'. Max@D6 will provide 'Dim Sum' and 'bites that include spicy chicken potsticker'. Across the road is the Ranelagh Takeaway, with little competition from Urban Health next door, providing amongst other healthy options, a 'cleansing juice', a 'matcha magic' or a 'strazler dazzler'. And if that isn't enough, Bodyfirst Nutrition, on the opposite corner, provides a 'wall of nut butter' to get you up and running. Rasoi, an 'Indian to go', claims it 'can make any sauce with prawn, chicken or lamb'. Facing on to the Triangle is DIEP at Home which specialises in Thai food.

SIGNATURE SAUCES AND PAN-FRIED POTATO CAKES

Returning to the main thoroughfare, just past Spar supermarket, was, until recently, Rio, a Brazilian restaurant ('the best barbecue in Ireland') where you could have the Rio Rodizio experience, which included trying fourteen different types of meat. In fact, you could 'eat as much meat as you like', flavoured with its 'signature sauce'. And if that wasn't enough you could also have 'unlimited tea and coffee'.

Past Rio, along by Redmond's Off-Licence, a long-established family business, there is a line of restaurants and takeaways including the Exchequer Wine Bar, where you can sample 'hickory-smoked baby port', and Kinara Kitchen, which specialises in Pakistani and Eastern cuisine. Here, they also serve 'aloo tikka', which are pan-friend Irish potato cakes. Nick's Coffee Company across the road claims to have the best coffee in Dublin. Pinocchio's Italian Restaurant and Wine Bar is beside and below the Luas stop in Ranelagh. Here you will enjoy the taste and flavour of Italian food.

11

'DRINK! DRINK! DRINK! TO EYES THAT ARE BRIGHT …'

FORMER CHEMIST'S 29 GINS

There is no shortage of pubs in Ranelagh, from The Hill at Old Mount Pleasant to McSorley's on the corner of Anna Villa. Both may have similar, old, traditional-style interiors, yet there is a gap of more than 100 years between them. The Hill is the original of the species, dating back to 1845. Many pubs have changed names over the years yet a lot of them have kept to the old, tried-and-trusted formula of tradition, which does much to copper-fasten the quaint village atmosphere of the area.

Despite its olde-worlde appearance and atmosphere, McSorley's has been trading as a pub on this site for only twenty-five years. Before that there was a pub called Durkan's on the same site. At one time, it was a chemist's shop. A reminder of this is its old front door and the word 'chemist' written into the mosaic floor at the corner entrance. Inside there are still hints of its former tenant, with shelves and small wall drawers reminiscent of a chemist's dispensary function. The interior decoration is done in dark-wood panelling. It is a comfortable pub with exceptional photography on the walls. And, crucially, this is a pub that has an excellent range of beers and spirits, including twenty-nine different types of gin!

THE EAGLE EYE OF JACK BIRCHALL

Birchall's, on the opposite corner of Anna Villa/Ranelagh, is another jewel and dates from 1850. It is one of the oldest surviving original pubs in Dublin. It was called McCauley's before it became James Birchall's in the 1970s. Later the 'James' was dropped, which is a pity as Declan Kiberd reminds us that author Bill Barick once described James Birchall as 'as eagle-eyed as a ship's captain navigating a choppy sea'. This is an old-school wooden bar with stained glass everywhere. It has quirky décor, including vintage clocks above doorways, bookshelves, armchairs by the fire, warm creamy-gold wallpaper, a half-door leaning into the snug, and old prints advertising bygone railways. All of them combine to make this a perfectly comfortable, atmospheric and authentic pub. Even Oscar Wilde got a look-in and this pub seems to be a popular venue for the academic and literary set. Flann O'Brien left a lasting legacy, being a one-time regular.

Smyth's at nos 75–77 is another old-school traditional pub with lots of dark timber which, together with Humphreys next door (occupying nos 79– 81), adds significantly in many ways to the attractive and slightly skewed and shaggy appearance of the terrace in the heart of Ranelagh. Smyth's was originally called Lyster's.

THE HABERDASHER AND THE SPIRIT GROCER

The full name 'Humphreys Grocer' over the entrance to Humphreys gives some hint of its provenance, but not the full story. There was a pub on the site in 1868 called Nolan's Pub. That was owned by a Mrs Eliza Nolan who ran it as a 'provision and spirit dealer'. Some of her neighbours included a Miss Jane Flint, haberdasher, and a Mr Charles Hedgelong.

This business survived and was bought by a Mr Francis Murtagh nearly thirty years later. He owned it until Timothy Humphreys bought it in 1910. Murtagh called it a 'family grocer and spirit dealer'. Humphreys previously had a pub on Thomas Street and there he used to bottle Guinness stout on the premises. His new venture continued to serve as a grocer's and a pub – a common practice in the business. Some even diversified into the undertaking business, such as The Morgue Pub in Templeogue. In *Thom's Directory* for the early decades of the twentieth century, Tim Humphreys is listed as a 'spirit grocer' at 12 and 13 Elm Grove, the site of the present-day pub. A sign survives in Humphreys: 'Tim Humphreys, family grocer, wine and spirit merchant, 12 and 13 Elm Grove, Ranelagh'. The pub was re-numbered, probably around 1932, as 79 and 81 Ranelagh.

FINEST OLD DUBLIN WHISKEY
AND 'INVALID' STOUT

In its early days, Humphreys was known as a 'gentleman's pub' – the type of establishment where a gentleman could go without losing face. This was also where they bottled ten-year-old Jameson whiskey, and they were able to claim their whiskeys had attained 'a universal reputation for excellence; stored and matured in sherry casks with the best properties developed, mellowed by age, and guaranteed free from all flavouring or deleterious ingredients. The Whiskey I offer will be found wholesome, of delicious bouquet and incomparably the best in the market.' Some of these whiskeys included Finest Old Dublin Whiskey, Power's Three Swallow, John Jameson & Son and Humphreys Celebrated Whiskey. They also sold Champagnes, Port (Rare Old, Finest Old, Very Old and Good Old), Sherry, Claret, Marsala and Burgundy. Some interesting ales and stouts were Bass & Co., Barley Wine (in baby bottles), Allsopp's Light Dinner Ale, O'Connell's Dublin Ale and Guinness's (Invalid Stout). In the grocery department where they sold 'teas', you were advised that 'the greatest care combined with long experience is exercised in selecting only the finest parcels from the large quantities shipped'. Furthermore, '… those only are purchased which have been previously tested by an eminent expert'. Some of these teas were 'Good Sound Tea', 'Excellent Value', 'Fine Medium Blend, Useful Family Tea', 'Choice Family Tea', 'Blended Assam', 'Good China Tea, or 'The Choicest India & Ceylon'. Humphreys also stocked 'sundries' such as pickles, sauces, tinned goods, biscuits, cakes and chocolates and so on. It also sold 'chandlery, toilet and fancy soap'.

FROM MYLES TO MOLLY

Brian O'Nolan (1911–66), otherwise known as Flann O'Brien or Myles na gCopaleen, used to frequent Humphreys and Birchall's. He was considered a major figure in mid-twentieth century Irish literary circles. He was a renowned satirist, his biting wit often expressed through his 'Cruiskeen Lawn' column in *The Irish Times*. His novels include *At Swim-Two-Birds* and *The Third Policeman*.

Tim Humphreys died in 1954. His widow, Molly Reilly, then ran the pub. After she died in 1970, the pub passed to her family. Humphreys Pub has been passed down through three generations of the family for over 100 years and consequently it is the oldest family-run business in the local pub trade and probably in general in Ranelagh.

THE PURSUIT OF 'HOPPINESS' AND THE HILL

The Taphouse Pub, facing the Triangle, was formerly well known as Russell's, with its roof-top beer garden on the first level overlooking the thoroughfare. This has been refurbished in recent years and the Russell's name has been deleted, with the emphasis now on it being a 'gastropub'. This is where young folks chat all about 'the lovely hoppiness' of some craft beer with names such as the 'Disappearing Fiver' or 'Show Us the Money' and sigh at the mere mention of the brioche burgers topped with quail's eggs.

Located at no. 1 Old Mount Pleasant, The Hill (formerly Butlers and then Kennedy's) is a landmark pub in the heart of Ranelagh. It is red-bricked in appearance, with its name shaped into the upper gable and spelt out in green neon lettering, illuminated at night by red-strip lighting around the edges, and never failing to attract. Nowadays, it's a gastropub offering fine food and craft beers such as the White Hag and Trouble Brewing from its twenty-two taps. The pub has been totally refurbished in recent years, yet it has retained that old-world atmosphere since it first opened its doors in 1845. The pub is a 'listed' one and through the vicissitudes of time and tides has admirably retained its Victorian stylings such as the old pumps, still in working order. It also has an old, large clock in the bar, only one of three such clocks in Dublin, still in working order over 100 years after first being installed. Today, The Hill is a reminder of the area's chequered past and is a welcome beacon to a weary traveller.

1910 – FROM GUINAN'S TO CORRIGAN'S

The Corrigan's Mount Pleasant Inn dates from 1910. Before that it was called Guinan's and that name is still carved in red stone high up on the front wall. Above it, '1910' is also carved into the top gable. It occupies a picturesque location on Mountpleasant Avenue beside the curved and attractive Bessborough Parade with the green dome of Rathmines Church in the background. The pub achieved a certain fame when a film on the young days of playwright Seán O'Casey called *Young Cassidy* was shot in the pub.

12

STOP THE LIGHTS! – STILL MORE LUMINARIES

HADRIEN'S RANELAGH

Besides the aforementioned luminaries and lesser lights that graced and continue to grace the stage and the highways and byways of Ranelagh, there are many other personalities that are associated with the area. For example, in March 2013, Lenny Abrahamson, Irish film and television director, filmed part of his movie *Frank* on Cowper Gardens and Park Drive of Ranelagh. Only Ranelagh would fit the bill, it was heard.

France's former cultural attaché to Ireland, the learned Hadrien Laroche, managed to write three books while based here. He recalled in 2014 that while in Dublin he stayed in Ranelagh for three months. He was staying 'down the street from that marvellous and hospitable home' of Seamus Deane, he fondly remembered. One of Laroche's favourite books is Seamus Deane's *Reading in the Dark* (1996).

CYPHERS AND THE LIGHTS OF RANELAGH

Still on matters literary, other residents include Eiléan Ní Chuilleanáin, one of the founders, with MacDara Woods and others, of the poetry magazine *Cyphers*. She was awarded the Patrick Kavanagh Award for her first collection of poetry, published in 1973. Her poems are noted for their use of history, mythology and religion and their sometimes elusive style. She is the daughter of the writer Eilís Dillon and is married to the poet MacDara Woods. Original and international in tone and scope, MacDara Woods has also engaged with the local environment of Dublin streets and scenes. He has been a presence in the Irish poetry scene since the 1970s. One of his books was called *Stopping the Lights in Ranelagh*.

Journalist John Mulholland, assistant editor of *The Guardian* and editor of *The Observer* (having been a reader of that paper since he was a teenager), was born in Ranelagh. He was one of seven children. He was awarded a degree in communications in 1983 by Dublin City University and later a master's in media and communications by California State University. Another media stalwart, Brendan O'Reilly, long-time RTÉ sports commentator, journalist, singer, songwriter, actor, author and Olympian, lived in Ranelagh for many years until his death in 2001.

WALKING THE LINE – HOTHOUSE FLOWERS AND ALTAN

On the music front, Liam Ó Maonlaí stands out, and has lived in Ranelagh for many years. He is best known for his band Hothouse Flowers. Born in Monkstown, Co. Dublin, he attended Gaelscoilleanna in Dublin, including Scoil Lorcáin and Coláiste Eoin, yet he attributes his love of the language to the influence of his father. He has won prizes for his skills on the bodhrán. His first band was called The Complex; when he left it, he went on to establish the renowned Hothouse Flowers in 1985. The remaining members of his former band renamed themselves My Bloody Valentine (from the horror film). O'Maonlaí was also politically active, campaigning with the Nuclear Free Future Movement and hosting events in Carnsore and Wexford town. The 2008 television documentary *Dambé: The Mali Project* tells the story of his 3,000-mile cross-cultural musical adventure with Paddy Keenan and friend, and features performances from the Festival au Désert.

It is not just the Hothouse Flowers that have a connection with Ranelagh. Another renowned Irish folk-music band, Altan (founded in Donegal in 1987 by Mairéad Ní Mhaonaigh and her husband Frankie Kennedy), has links via band member Ciaran Tourish. He hails from Buncrana in east Co. Donegal. Although Ciaran started playing the tin whistle at an early age, he soon took up the fiddle under the guidance of local legendary fiddler and teacher Dinny McLaughlin. In addition to his mastery of the dance-music tradition, Ciaran's quick ear, and his love of harmony and counterpoint have led to him being in demand as a valued collaborator on non-Altan and even non-Irish music projects with a wide range of musicians and singers. He released his first solo recording, *Down the Line*, in 2005, featuring guest musicians Arty McGlynn, Paul Brady, Maura O'Connell, Tim O'Brien, Alison Krauss and Jerry Douglas among others. He continues to play and tour with Altan, which is still going strong after an incredible thirty years.

TENNIS PLAYERS AND FOLEY'S ASIA

Ronan Sheehan is an Irish novelist, short-story writer and essayist. He was an early member of the Irish Writers' Co-operative and its secretary from 1975 to 1983. He received the Rooney Prize for Irish Literature in 1984. His background is interesting, as he was trained as a lawyer and specialised in copyright law. Before that he was educated at Ranelagh's very own Gonzaga College, and later at UCD and the Incorporated Law Society. Among his writings are *Tennis Players* (1977), *Boy with an Injured Eye* (1983) and *Foley's Asia* (1999). Neil Jordan, the Irish film maker, called *Foley's Asia*, 'A meditation on arms, oppression and empire, [offering] a unique insight into [the] Irish and Indian colonial experience.' *The Heart of the City* (1988) won many awards, including the Hennessey Literary Award for short stories. He also won the Arts Council Award. Moreover, he worked on the political and cultural journal *Crane Bag*. A passionate advocate of the Latin poet Catullus, he edited *The Irish Catullus: One Gentleman from Verona*.

JUNE LEVINE AND SISTERS TO BELFAST

June Levine (1931–2008) was a journalist, novelist and feminist who played a central part in the Irish women's movement. She was born and raised in a Jewish family in Dublin, and wrote her first articles for *The Irish Times* when she was still a teenager. At the age of 18, she married Kenneth Mesbur, a Jewish medical student from Canada. She moved to Ontario and had three children by him. However, the marriage broke down and she returned with her children to Dublin, where she worked as a journalist. She edited the *Irish Women's Journal*, and worked as a researcher for RTÉ for five years. She wrote two best-selling books, *Sisters*, a personal history of the feminist movement, and (with Lyn Madden) *Lyn: A Story of Prostitution*. She also wrote a novel, *A Season of Weddings*. Within the Irish women's movement, she campaigned alongside figures such as Mary Kenny, Margaret Gaj and Mary Maher. In 1971 she boarded with other feminists, including Mary Kenny and Nell McCafferty (another long-time Ranelagh resident), the so-called 'contraceptive train', and they travelled to Belfast to buy condoms. In 1999, June Levine married her partner of thirty years, psychiatrist Professor Ivor Browne.

PSYCHIATRY AND CHOPPING BRAINS

Eminent psychiatrist Ivor Browne has been a pioneer of and a central figure in mental-health matters in Ireland for decades. He is another long-time resident of Ranelagh. Today, he is a well-known figure often seen rambling around Ranelagh. He is known for his opposition to traditional psychiatry, and his scepticism about psychiatric drugs. Born in 1929 in Sandycove, Co. Dublin, he said that he was a dreamy, often miserable child. He attended secondary school at Blackrock College, where he discovered jazz music, and began playing the trumpet. After Blackrock College, he gained admission to the Royal College of Surgeons. He said that his intention was to become a jazz musician and that he only took up medicine to please his parents. According to Browne, his professor of medicine in the Richmond Hospital told him, 'You're only fit to be an obstetrician or a psychiatrist.' He had little interest in general medicine, and decided to become a psychiatrist. He started his internship in a neurosurgical unit, where he assisted a surgeon. He said of his work there, 'Nearly every Saturday morning one or two patients would be sent down from Grangegorman to have their brains chopped ... this was the major lobotomy procedure ... where burr holes were drilled on each side of the temples and a blunt instrument inserted to sever the frontal lobes almost completely from the rest of the brain'. Browne went on to work both in the UK and in the US. He was awarded a scholarship to study public and community mental health in Harvard. After returning to Ireland, he became the fifth medical superintendent of Grangegorman Mental Hospital (St Brendan's) and was made professor of psychiatry at UCD and chief psychiatrist of the Eastern Health Board.

THE WONDER EYE AND THELONIOUS SPHERE MONK

Colm Tóibín, award-winning author and friend of Browne's late wife, June Levine, said of him, 'He's just a good doctor, a kind man who would get up in the middle of the night for people. There's an aura off him which is almost holy.' Sebastian Barry echoed that, saying his experience with Browne was 'transformative' in his creative life when he accompanied him to Grangegorman after a fire broke out there. What he witnessed inspired his *Secret Scripture*. Tom Murphy also cited his influence. In 2017 Professor Brown was the subject of an Alan Gilsenan documentary, *Meetings with Ivor* (previously screened as *The Wonder Eye*), which captures the essence of a remarkable human being. 'The truth is there is no therapy. There is nothing *I* can do for you that changes you,' he said. 'I can provide the context of safety, but they [the patients] have to face the pain'. He wrote a memoir, *Music and Madness,* which shows that, besides psychiatry, music is the other guiding passion in his life. Jazz, for him, is the music of the dispossessed and the excluded. One of his favourites artists is the American jazz pianist and composer Thelonious Sphere Monk, equally innovative, challenging and unorthodox. Precisely what is needed – medicine for the mind.

FURTHER READING

Ball, F.E., *History of the County Dublin* (Alexander Thom: Dublin, 1902–17)

Barry, Michael, *Victorian Dublin Revealed* (Andalus Press: Dublin, 2011)

Bourke, Angela, *Maeve Brennan: Homesick in New York* (Jonathan Cape: London, 2005)

Byrne, Charles Artaud, *Ranelagh. The Irish Warlord* (Tate Publishing: Mustang, Oklahoma, 2008)

Curtis, Maurice, *Rathmines* (The History Press: Dublin, 2011)

Curtis, Maurice, *Portobello* (The History Press: Dublin, 2012)

Curtis, Maurice, *Rathgar: A History* (The History Press: Dublin, 2015)

Daly, Mary; Pearson, Peter and Hearn, Mona, *Dublin's Victorian Houses* (A&A Farmar: Dublin, 1998)

De Courcey, S. & J., *Church of the Holy Name, Beechwood Avenue, Ranelagh, Dublin: History and Guide* (Dublin (N.D.))

Donnelly, Most Rev. Nicholas, *A Short History of Some Dublin Parishes, part 6: Parish of St Nicholas Without, Francis Street, section 3: Parish of Rathmines* (Catholic Truth Society of Ireland: Dublin, 1909)

Dublin City Council, *The Georgian Squares of Dublin* (DCC: Dublin, 2006)

Igoe, Vivien, *A Literary Guide to Dublin* (Methuen: London, 1999)

Joyce, Weston St John, *The Neighbourhood of Dublin* (M.H. Gill: Dublin, 1939)

Kelly, Deirdre, *Four Roads to Dublin* (The O'Brien Press: Dublin, 1995)

Mac Aonghusa, Brian, *The Harcourt Street Line: Back to Track* (Columba Press: Dublin, 2003)

O'Donnell, E.E., *Father Browne's Dublin* (Gill & MacMillan: Dublin, 1996)

O'Maitiu, Seamus, *Dublin's Suburban Towns 1834–1930* (Four Courts Press: Dublin, 2003)

Roundtree, Susan, *Ranelagh in Pictures* (A. & A. Farmer: Dublin, 2009)

Sweeney, Clair L., *The Rivers of Dublin* (Dublin City Council: Dublin, 1991)